the G L A S G

visitor guide

Colin Baxter Photography, Grantown-on-Spey, Scotland

CONTENTS

Kelvingrove Art Gallery & Museum

HOW TO USE THIS GUIDE

Entries in the Glasgow Visitor Guide are arranged alphabetically, and contain practical information on facilities, opening times, admission, directions, contact telephone number and website plus a short description. A typical entry looks like this one for Glasgow School of Art (below).

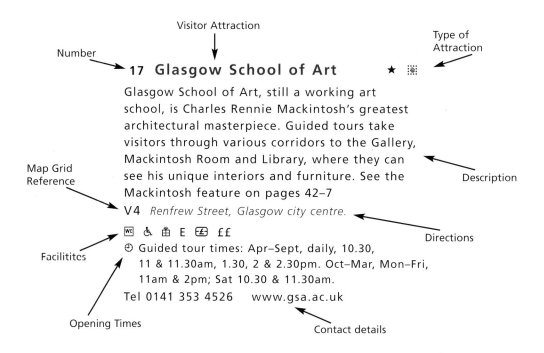

Number

Visitor Attraction

Type of Attraction

17 Glasgow School of Art ★ ▒

Glasgow School of Art, still a working art school, is Charles Rennie Mackintosh's greatest architectural masterpiece. Guided tours take visitors through various corridors to the Gallery, Mackintosh Room and Library, where they can see his unique interiors and furniture. See the Mackintosh feature on pages 42–7

Description

Map Grid Reference

V4 *Renfrew Street, Glasgow city centre.*

Directions

WC & ⌂ E £ ££

🕐 Guided tour times: Apr–Sept, daily, 10.30, 11 & 11.30am, 1.30, 2 & 2.30pm. Oct–Mar, Mon–Fri, 11am & 2pm; Sat 10.30 & 11.30am.

Tel 0141 353 4526   www.gsa.ac.uk

Facilitites

Opening Times

Contact details

About the Symbols
A number of symbols have been used throughout the book to represent types of attractions, facilities and whether the entry is associated with the National Trust for Scotland or Historic Scotland. You can find a list of these symbols on the inside cover of this book.

Using the Maps
All entries are clearly marked on colour-coded maps (on pages 18 & 19, 20 & 21 & 64) using the reference number next to the title (in the case of Glasgow School of Art, 17). You can also use the map grid reference (V4) to find the location quickly.

Using the Indexes
Two indexes at the back of the book provide easy reference; the first is ordered by region and type of attraction, and the second is alphabetical by title.

Special Text
A number of special features appear throughout the guide, which highlight areas and places of historical interest, events and attractions.

VISITOR INFORMATION

Tourist Information Centres offer a wealth of information to anyone visiting Glasgow and the surrounding area. They can advise visitors on events, attractions, festivals and activities. Passes can also be arranged for transport on buses and the subway system. The centres carry a selection of books, guidebooks, maps and souvenirs. You can also book accommodation in Glasgow and throughout Scotland through the centres and some offer a service for foreign currency exchange.

TOURIST INFORMATION CENTRES

Glasgow
11 George Square
Glasgow
G2 1 DY
Tel: 0141 204 4400
Email: enquiries@seeglasgow.com
Web: www.seeglasgow.com
Open: all year

Abington
Welcome Break Motorway Service Area
Junction 13, M74
Abington
ML12 6RG
Tel: 01864 502436
Email: abington@seeglasgow.com
Open: all year

Balloch
Balloch Road
Balloch
G83 8LQ
Tel: 08707 200607
Email: info@balloch.visitscotland.com
Open: Apr-Oct

Balloch
National Park Gateway Centre
Balloch G83 8LQ
Tel: 08707 200631
Email: info@lochlomond.visitscotland.com
Open: Apr-Oct

Dumbarton
A82 Northbound
Dumbarton
G82 2TZ
Tel: 08707 200612
Email: info@milton.visitscotland.com
Open: all year

Glasgow Airport
Tourist Information Desk
Glasgow International Airport
Paisley PA3 2ST
Tel: 0141 848 4440
Email: airport@seeglasgow.com
Open: all year

Hamilton
Road Chef Services
M74 Northbound
Hamilton
ML3 6JW
Tel: 01698 285590
Email: hamilton@seeglasgow.com
Open: all year

Helensburgh
Clock Tower
The Pier
Helensburgh
G84 7NY
Tel: 08707 200615
Email: info@helensburgh.visitscotland.com
Open: Apr-Oct

Lanark
Horsemarket
Ladyacre Road
Lanark ML11 7LQ
Tel: 01555 661661
Email: lanark@seeglasgow.com
Open: all year

Paisley
9a Gilmour Street
Paisley PA1 1DD
Tel: 0141 889 0711
Email: paisley@seeglasgow.com
Open: all year

GLASGOW

Less than an hour by road or rail separates Glasgow from Edinburgh. But such close proximity belies the very real differences that exist between these two great cities. Maybe it is something in the West Coast air, but Glasgow can feel much closer to even Dublin than to the nation's capital. However that is only on first acquaintance. As you will soon discover, Glasgow is not really like anywhere else on the planet.

It is probably easier to say what Glasgow is not, and hopefully lay a few myths to rest in the process. It is no longer an industrial city and has not been for some time. Its old, well-worn claim to fame – that of being the 'Second City of the Empire' – had begun to disappear years before the Empire itself suffered the same fate.

The period of readjustment that followed the loss of its key industries like shipbuilding was slow and drawn-out. For a while the city appeared to lose its way and seemed unsure of its role in a changed world. There are certainly poignant reminders of the past as a ride to the top of the Millennium Tower reveals. Here, looking down from this space-age structure beside the Clyde you get an unparalleled sense of where the city has been and where it might be heading. Downstream the riverbanks

are cut with massive slanting docks, built by men who clearly believed the city would build ships forever. They have long been silent. Yet springing up amongst them are a growing band of futuristic buildings like the Science Centre and the so-called 'Armadillo', which houses all the big trade shows and exhibitions. Like all cities there are scenes of the future and scenes of dereliction. Only in Glasgow would you find them quite so cheek-by-jowl.

So yes, there are still some rough edges and a good sprinkling of urban grit if that's what you want, but the core of Glasgow is transformed. Today it is a thoroughly modern, design-conscious city whose face has been scrubbed clean of any last traces of industrial grime. For anyone expecting a cloth-capped theme park that may prove disappointing. For the rest of us, however, Glasgow is simply a great place to get to know. Despite all the tough times, it never lost its sense of humour and to this day remains a true original – a spontaneous free spirit among cities that is hard to define.

EARLY HISTORY

Glasgow was founded by St Mungo in the sixth century and evolved slowly as a small religious community. Very little is known about St Mungo, except that

Glasgow Green & the River Clyde, City Centre

he first came here with the Christian missionary, St Ninian. It is said that he was inspired by an angel to return and build a small wooden church on the banks of the Molendinar Burn close to the River Clyde.

It seems some sort of cult grew up around Mungo, who became Glasgow's patron saint. His following also included his mother, who strangely became known as St Enoch and whose name lives on in a glass-domed shopping mall at the bottom of Buchanan Street. St Mungo meanwhile features on the city's coat of arms along with a salmon, a tree, a bird and a bell. The city's motto 'Let Glasgow Flourish' is supposed to represent Mungo's ability to work for the common good.

As for Glasgow's name, there are a number of theories. Some claim the church was set up in a place called 'deschu' – later changed to 'glashu' – which translates as 'dear place'. Others say it is a combination of two Gaelic words, 'glas' meaning green and 'cau' meaning hollow or valley. Over time these have combined to form the city's epithet of 'Dear Green Place'.

The earliest recorded mention of Glasgow was not until 1114 when the first bishop was appointed. This led to the building of a stone Cathedral some 20 years later. In 1190 it burnt down, but was quickly replaced by a much more substantial Cathedral, the largest in Scotland after St Andrews.

Despite many extensions since, it is still possible to pick up a faint sense of medieval Glasgow if you stand inside the Cathedral – a sense that is lost the moment you step outside.

In 1451 Glasgow University was founded within the Cathedral grounds. It was the second in the country after St Andrews, and soon moved to its own site nearby where it remained until the mid 19th century. It then decamped to the West End, in part to escape the squalor and pollution that plagued the city centre at the time.

In 1492 the town gained its first Archbishop, Robert Blacader, whose diocese stretched all the way down to the Solway Firth. This underlined Glasgow's status as an ecclesiastical centre. In terms of economic importance or political clout, however, it remained a relative backwater throughout the Middle Ages. During the sixteenth century Glasgow developed along its principal street – the High Street – which ran south from the Cathedral to Glasgow Cross, and acquired its first stone bridge over the Clyde.

By the early 1600s, this growing market town had a population of around 7000, second only to Ayr on the West Coast. It was a town of tradesmen – of tailors, bonnet-makers, coopers and skinners all organised into their respective guilds. The Union of the Crowns in 1603 increased trade with England, particularly in linen and yarn. Later King James VI and I encouraged West Coast Scots to settle in Ulster to help keep order there, and this strengthened Glasgow's trading links across the Irish Sea. Glasgow also traded with the Baltic States and Norway, shipping timber, flax and iron ore, but the scale was miniscule compared to the trans-Atlantic trade with America and the Caribbean that was to develop later during the eighteenth century. Before then Scotland continued to look east for its trading links, and this inevitably favoured North Sea ports such as Dundee and Leith and not Glasgow. Besides, Glasgow's location appeared far too in-land to operate properly as a port. Here the Clyde was just 15 inches deep at low tide and ships had to anchor miles downstream while their cargoes were transferred onto small boats and rafts for the final leg of the journey.

The accession of William of Orange in 1688 ushered in a more peaceful period of history when minds turned from religious discord to commerce. Yet Scotland felt, not for the last time, constrained by its southern neighbour and in particular by the all-powerful East India Company in London. Earlier laws had sought to prevent the Scots trading directly with the English colonies. Glasgow responded by building a harbour 20 miles downriver called Port Glasgow in order to exploit whatever trading opportunities there might be. A much grander scheme to circumvent the English was unveiled in 1695, when it was decided to set up the 'Company of Scotland Trading to Africa and the Indies' – a direct rival to the East India Company. With a third of its investment coming from Glasgow, the new company tried

The Tolbooth Steeple lies at the southern end of the High Street at Glasgow Cross. Built in 1626, it was Glasgow's first town hall and jail.

to establish a colony in Panama that would act as a trading post and give Scotland free access to the Atlantic and the Pacific, and the markets of the New World. Known as the Darien Scheme, it proved an unmitigated disaster. It left the country virtually bankrupt and helped push it towards joining England under the Act of Union of 1707.

UP IN SMOKE

Humbled by the Darien disaster, and humiliated by the Act, which Glasgow bitterly opposed, it took a while for the city to realise that political union represented a golden opportunity.

As part of Britain, Glasgow could for the first time trade with the colonies as freely as Liverpool or Bristol.

First the city had to regain its self-esteem and composure. The writer Daniel Defoe, who was then in Scotland as an English spy, reported civil unrest. 'The rabble are now fully masters of the town', he wrote after the Lord Provost's house was stormed in 1707. Order was restored within a fortnight and Defoe went on to praise Glasgow as 'one of cleanest, most beautiful and best-built cities of Great Britain.' He described the five principal streets lined with stone houses, supported up to the first floor on Doric columns with arches opening onto shops.

The cash crop that gave Glasgow its first taste of real money was tobacco. Although a cargo of Caribbean tobacco had been landed as early as 1647, the real boom happened over a century later when Glasgow's ships could cross the Atlantic faster than those from any English port. In the 25 years up to the outbreak of the American War of Independence in 1775, the city took around half the tobacco produced in Maryland and Virginia. Up to 80% of this was re-exported to mainland Europe, making a number of the city's merchants Scotland's first millionaires in the process. Contemporary reports described these 'Tobacco Lords' strutting down the only pavement in town in the Trongate, resplendent in their scarlet coats, full-bottomed wigs and cocked hats. Whenever they travelled to Edinburgh they no doubt provoked considerable envy.

The tobacco was housed in cavernous warehouses in what is now called the Merchant City. The street names in the area recall these early tycoons. Glassford Street, for example, was named after John Glassford who owned 25 ships and was turning over £500,000 a year by 1760 (around £60 million in today's money). There was a mini property boom as the merchants migrated a few streets west to turn George Square into the most fashionable address in town. Meanwhile Scotland's leading architects of the day, the Adam brothers, were commissioned to build a number of important public buildings nearby, notably the Trades Hall and the Assembly Rooms.

The run on tobacco came to an abrupt end with the American War of Independence. The plantation owners simply went direct to the European importers, cutting out Glasgow altogether. Trading with the Caribbean continued, however, and cotton soon joined the list of commodities being traded, which included tobacco, spices, sugar – and slaves.

FULL STEAM AHEAD

By the end of the eighteenth century there was a well-established tradition of hand-loom weaving in what is now the city's East End. But it took the industrial revolution to transform this cottage industry into something much bigger. If the looms could be powered

University of Glasgow

somehow and installed in factories, textiles could be produced on a massive scale. Other manufacturing centres in Britain were gearing up for the revolution, but Glasgow had a head start, with wealthy entrepreneurs willing to invest in new industries and a university pushing at the boundaries of scientific knowledge.

In Glasgow the Scottish Enlightenment saw its practical manifestation thanks to men like James Watt. Born in Greenock, Watt had been educated at the University, or Glasgow College as it was then known, and later worked there helping to repair mathematical instruments. In the University laboratory he studied ways to harness the power of steam. The final breakthrough came to him one Sunday morning in 1765 while he was walking across Glasgow Green.

The steam engine was born and with it the industrial revolution.

Textiles needed dyeing, and inspired by a new technique to whiten cloth, Charles Tennant built the St Rollox works within 450 metres of the Cathedral. It was the biggest chemical factory in the world and did nothing for the environment. There were huge holding tanks full of urine – the cheapest form of ammonia – and a chimney that pumped out great clouds of sulphureous fumes.

To try and improve matters the chimney was extended to 133 metres and became a prominent city landmark known as Tennant's Stalk. In practice it merely diffused the pollution over a wider area. By 1879 the workforce at St Rollox had grown to 3000, many of them unskilled Irish immigrants on just £40 a year. This was the ugly face of capitalism where workers were

Finnieston Quay Crane

ruthlessly exploited and working conditions were often appalling.

The city's population of 83,000 in 1801 saw a five-fold increase over the next 50 years. The urban drift from the countryside turned into a stampede. First came the Highlanders who had been forced out of their crofts and replaced with sheep during the Highland Clearances that began in the 1820s. Then in even greater numbers came the Irish, desperately fleeing the potato famines of the early 1840s. In 1848, at the peak of this influx, it was claimed that up to 1000 Irish immigrants a week were arriving in Glasgow. The effect was all too predictable – huge overcrowding leading to inner-city slums and low wages and periodic bouts of mass unemployment as too many people chased not enough jobs.

By then the cotton-spinning industry had long since been replaced by heavy industry. The city's hinterland of Lanarkshire, Ayrshire and Stirlingshire had rich deposits of coal and ironstone, and by the 1830s new, higher temperature blast furnaces were producing high quality Scottish iron. Iron and steel were in demand by the growing railways, which required a steady supply of rolling stock and carriages which were hammered out in the city's engineering works.

Then came shipbuilding – Glasgow's most famous industry and source of its industrial pride. Various factors combined to make Glasgow the shipbuilding capital of the world.

As well as ready access to iron and steel, its engineering prowess was well proven. As early as 1812, Henry Bell had produced the *Comet* there – Europe's first practical, sea-going steamer. In the second half of the nineteenth century demand for steamers grew and reached its peak in 1870.

By then Glasgow was producing over two thirds of all the iron ships in the world. This heyday was already starting to fade by the outbreak of the First World War in 1914. Even so, that year some 40 firms, mostly family-run and based in Govan, produced more ships than the whole of Germany or the USA. To cope with demand, more and more docks, including Kingston Dock and the massive Queen's Dock, were cut into the banks of the Clyde. With more space to berth ships, Glasgow became the home of many famous shipping lines.

The shipowners themselves were symbols of the city's wealth and often generous supporters of the arts. The likes of Kelvingrove Art Gallery are brimming with their bequests. The greatest benefactor of all was William Burrell, a shipping magnate who began his vast, eclectic collection in the 1880s. A century later it was finally displayed to the public in the grounds of Pollok House. The fabulous Burrell Collection was instrumental in winning Glasgow the coveted title of European City of Culture in 1990.

By the mid 19th century, Glasgow's population had overtaken Edinburgh's and its growth showed no signs of slowing down. To house the incomers, rows of sub-standard tenements sprang up where the villas and gardens of the Tobacco Lords had once stood. In 1848 there was a bad outbreak of cholera and scenes of civil unrest. Faced with large crowds of hungry, unemployed men gathering on Glasgow Green, the city fathers were forced to take notice. The water supply was improved and slum clearance began in 1866. But the city's problems were attracting a great deal of negative comment. 'I did not believe,' wrote one social commentator after a visit to the East End, 'that so large an amount of filth, crime, misery and disease existed in one spot in any civilised country.'

THE SOCIAL MIX

Meanwhile, those that could afford to were moving steadily westwards to escape from the downtown squalor and overcrowding. The first wave pushed the city's boundaries to Blythswood Hill and regency developments like Blythswood Square. The second took them to the West End. This middle-class migration was helped by the opening of the Great Western Road in 1841 which connected the exclusive suburb of Kelvinside to the city centre. Others moved south of the river to smart terraces and south-side villas designed by the celebrated Victorian architect, Alexander 'Greek' Thomson.

At the same time other immigrant communities were developing. There

had been a Jewish settlement of mainly Dutch and German Jews as early as 1820. This had grown to almost 6000 by the outbreak of the First World War due to émigrés fleeing the Russian pogroms. Scotland's first synagogue opened in Garnethill, just north of the city, in 1879. At first many Jewish families settled in the Gorbals, before moving south to Govanhill, Queen's Park and more recently Newton Mearns. From the 1920s their place in the Gorbals was being filled by Asian Muslims from the Punjab. Their numbers swelled after the Second World War when Pakistani and Indian families arrived to escape high unemployment at home. Many became drivers and ticket collectors on the city's trams, buses and underground, others opened corner stores and restaurants. To this day Glasgow has some of the finest curry houses in Britain.

There were also the Italians, whose influence was out of all proportion to their numbers. Today there are around 30,000 'Italo-Scozzesi' in Scotland, a good third of them living in or around Glasgow. Finding most of the manual jobs already taken by the Irish, the Italian immigrants of the early twentieth century turned to selling ice cream and fish and chips. The locals were soon hooked and a network of 'chippies' and ice cream parlours began spreading throughout the city and beyond. Few families were as successful as the Giulianis of Glasgow who had a chain of over 60 cafés by 1900. Later, when the seaside resort of Largs became undisputed capital of the 'Costa del Clyde', the Nardinis opened a huge Art Deco café there that still pulls in the crowds today. Later generations of West Coast Italians turned to other professions including acting, among them Tom Conti, Peter Capaldi and Daniella Nardini.

TWENTIETH-CENTURY BLUES

The city's shipyards and engineering works were hit by an economic slump in 1908 and the ensuing job losses gave rise to increased militancy among the trade unions. During this period the industrial Clyde was known as 'Red Clydeside' when the workers' struggle was championed by the newly formed Labour party. The First World War gave the industry a temporary boost, supplying the navy and replacing merchant ships that had been sunk. But in 1918 the engineering workers went on strike for a 40-hour week and this culminated in a riot outside the City Chambers in George Square. With the Russian Revolution then in full swing the authorities moved fast and locked up the ringleaders. Four years later, the Labour party won ten of the city's 15 seats at the General Election. Glasgow became a socialist stronghold and still remains a bastion of 'Old Labour'.

Increased foreign competition and the Great Depression of the 1930s slowly crippled shipbuilding on the Clyde. There was another temporary uplift during the Second World War, and building such luxury liners as the *QE2* and the *Queen Mary* gave the city's self-esteem a quick boost. To be 'Clyde-built' was something to be proud of, but by the early 1970s it was clear the industry was in sharp decline.

For a while Glasgow turned its back on the Clyde, which grew eerily quiet. The M8 motorway that snakes through the city centre on stilts seemed all the louder by comparison. Before allowing the motorway to split the city in two, the City Council had been steadily decanting the citizens out of their decaying tenements into outlying New Towns like Cumbernauld and East Kilbride. The city's population shrank to around 700,000 and suffice to say

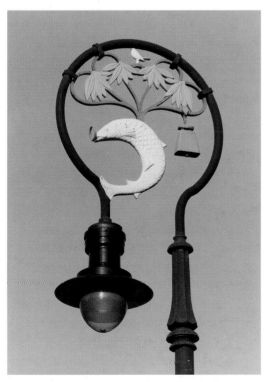

The emblems on Glasgow's coat of arms, the bird, the tree, the fish and the bell, represent legend's from the life of St. Mungo

St Andrew's Cathedral & the St Enoch Centre across the River Clyde

not everyone was pleased to swap their old community for a tower block. But having left the river to rest in peace, the city planners are now determined to breathe fresh life into the area. The ships and heavy industry may have all but gone for good, but the plan is to revitalise the Clyde with offices, shops and riverside apartments. The Science Centre at the Pacific Quay on the south bank and the 'Armadillo' opposite are just the start.

FROM SHIPS TO SHOPPING

By 1912 the population of Greater Glasgow had passed a million. The city fathers continued to tackle the problems of poor housing, but the money was always tight. Post-war reconstruction schemes were often postponed or abandoned due to a lack of funds, brought on by high unemployment and the failure to attract new industries. To the outside world Glasgow came to symbolise inner-city deprivation. Best-selling books like *No Mean City*, published in 1935, were filled with graphic descriptions of the 'razor gangs' who fought each other for control of the streets. The picture of violence and poverty was frequently exaggerated and even sentimentalised at times, but it created an image that has been very hard to shake off, especially when the media continued to pander to people's preconceptions. According to Billy Connolly, who used to be a Clydeside welder before he turned to comedy, documentary film makers

16

didn't always let the facts get in the way of a good story. 'When short of evidence of marauding gangs terrorising the wide-eyed and innocent populace [they] were not above slipping some unemployed youths a couple of bob to impersonate the same.' This may have boosted ratings, but it hardly encouraged anyone from outside the city to come and see for themselves.

Finally in the early 1980s the City Council decided to launch a campaign to tell people of the city's new image. With the slogan 'Glasgow's Miles Better' and with 'Mr Happy' as its mascot, it was a gift to local comedians. And yet it slowly became clear that more than just a PR initiative was taking place. The city centre took on a fresh, scrubbed-up appearance as its blackened buildings were sandblasted clean. All the hard work paid off and the city was named European City of Culture in 1990. For other cities this would be no big deal – the year Florence won hardly anyone noticed – but for Glasgow it was proof that its new-found belief in itself was something others shared. Nine years later this was reaffirmed when Glasgow was named European City of Architecture & Design.

Today's Glasgow comes across as cool and self-confident – a place with no need to prove itself. It has a buzz, an attitude about it that other cities simply don't have. What it may lack on the Heritage

trail – think of Edinburgh Castle or the Beefeaters outside the Tower of London – it more than makes up for with its ever-growing mix of bars, clubs and restaurants. And not only can you eat and drink supremely well, the shopping is second only to London – a retail heaven packed with flagship stores and quirky, one-off boutiques. On party nights 'dressed-up Glasgow' can rival Milan, the self-appointed style capital of Europe. Except, that is, in one crucial respect. Unlike the Milanesi, most Glaswegians seem genetically incapable of taking themselves too seriously.

Tom Bruce-Gardyne

The Music Room, House for an Art Lover. This elegant building opened in 1996 and was constructed from Charles Rennie Mackintosh's original designs of 1901

ATTRACTIONS IN GLASGOW

1 Bellahouston Park ♣ ❄

This large park covers 169 acres and was opened to the public in 1896. The famous Empire exhibition of 1938 was held in the park although only one building remains, the Palace of Art, which is now a sports centre. Another building to feature in the park is Charles Rennie Mackintosh's House for an Art Lover. This modern construction is based on Mackintosh's original designs of 1901, and opened here in 1996. It is now a centre for visual arts and conference venue. (See separate entries on pages 37 & 38.) Several notable gardens are located in the park, including a walled garden containing a collection of plants gathered by a local nineteenth-century plant collector, Peter Bar. The park also provides a wide variety of sporting facilities with bowling greens, an 18-hole 'pitch & putt' course, orienteering course and play areas. A ranger service is available and major events and activities are held throughout the year.

18 *Dumbreck Road, three miles SW of Glasgow City Centre, adjacent to J23 and J24 of the M8.*

🅿 ⓦⓒ ♿ 🐕 🏕 👫 FREE

⊙ Park; all year, dawn to dusk.
Walled garden: closes one hour before park.
Specific facilities within the park are subject to opening times and admission charges.

Tel 0141 427 0558
www.glasgow.gov.uk

Charing Cross Mansions

2 Botanic Gardens ❄

These gardens are best known for their tropical collections including the national collections of dendrobium orchids, begonias and tree ferns.The historic Kibble Palace glasshouse is one of Glasgow's best known landmarks. Formerly a private conservatory, it was relocated here in 1873. It now houses the collection of temperate plants. The gardens also have an arboretum, herbaceous borders, herb garden, rose and scented garden and play area for children. See feature on page 23.

K11 *Corner of Great Western Road and Queen Margaret Drive NW of Glasgow city centre.*

ⓦⓒ ♿ E 🏕 FREE

⊙ Garden: 7am–dusk.
Glasshouses: winter, daily, 10am–4.15pm; summer, 10am–4.45pm.
Kibble Palace closed until Summer 2006 for major refurbishment.

Tel 0141 334 2422
www.glasgow.gov.uk

3 Burrell Collection 🏛

The Burrell Collection, housed within the grounds of Pollok Country Park, is a diverse collection of over 9000 art exhibits. Sir William Burrell was heir to an extensive merchant fleet and a self-trained art collector. When he and his brother sold the business in 1916, he was able to build up his remarkable collection, which was eventually given to the city of Glasgow in 1944. Today his collection is housed in a purpose-built gallery which opened in 1983 and draws attention from around the world. See feature on page 24.

J7 *Pollok County Park, Pollokshaws Road, three miles S of Glasgow city centre.*

🅿 ⓦⓒ ♿ 🐕 ✕ 🍴 E 🎧 💳 FREE

⊙ Mon–Thur & Sat 10am–5pm;
Fri & Sun 11am–5pm.
Closed 25, 26 Dec, 31 Dec(pm) and 1, 2 Jan.

Tel 0141 287 2550
www.glasgowmuseums.com

THE BOTANIC GARDENS

The Botanic Gardens is one of over 70 parks within the city boundaries, which include Glasgow Green, Kelvingrove and Pollok Country Park, home of the Burrell Collection. It was the Victorians who realised that city dwellers needed a respite from overcrowded living conditions caused by the industrial revolution. The first was Kelvingrove beside the River Kelvin, whose gardens were laid out by Sir Joseph Paxton, who also designed London's Crystal Palace. Kelvingrove remains a much-loved place to escape to whenever the weather's warm.

Also in the West End are the nearby Botanic Gardens, which were originally run by the Royal Botanical Institution to supply plants for classes in botany and medicine at Glasgow University. When the Gardens moved to their present site in 1842 the public were occasionally admitted for the princely sum of one penny.

Their outstanding feature is the Kibble Palace, a magnificent glasshouse whose domed roof has been a prominent landmark since it was shipped here in 1873. It had been the conservatory of the Glasgow businessman, John Kibble, at his garden on Loch Long.

At Kelvinside it was originally used as a concert hall and meeting place and was where two British Prime Ministers, Gladstone and Disraeli, both gave addresses as rectors of the university.

Covering an area of over 2000 square metres, the Kibble Palace is one of the largest glasshouses in Britain and houses a wide variety of tree ferns from Australia and New Zealand and plants from the Americas, Africa and Asia. The Botanic Gardens also boast a fine collection of tropical orchids and begonias.

In the summer of 2006, after a major restoration off site, the Kibble Palace is to re-open along with its west wing which has been closed for 12 years.

Two special features are planned, one displaying plant treasures from islands such as the Canaries and St. Helena, the other showing insectivorous plants and how the plant and animal kingdoms interact.

Outside you can stroll along the various paths through formal gardens including the recently installed World Rose Garden, or beside the River Kelvin. The gardens are open every day from 7am until dusk.

THE BURRELL COLLECTION AND POLLOK COUNTRY PARK

The Glasgow shipping magnate William Burrell (1861-1958) made his fortune during the First World War and started an extraordinary magpie collection of art and artefacts.' In 1944 he gave the whole lot to the City of Glasgow on condition that it was to be displayed away from the city's then polluted atmosphere. It was not until 1983 that the entire collection of around 9000 works of art was finally unveiled in a purpose-built gallery in the grounds of Pollok Country Park 3 miles southwest of the city centre. Burrell's legacy can be seen immediately in the building's painstaking design which incorporates stonework from his house at Hutton Castle in the Borders and from other historic homes. Once inside, the visitor is entranced by a wealth of art – from ancient civilisations such as Egyptian, Indian and Chinese through to the art of the Middle East, featuring prayer rugs and ceramics. But it was medieval European art which was one of Burrell's obsessions and this is represented through stained glass, armour, glassware and tapestries which are a centrepiece of the collection. Burrell was also acutely aware of the movements in more contemporary art and collected widely. Among the many paintings are works by Rembrandt, Degas and Manet as well as Rodin's famous sculpture, 'The Thinker'. Pollok Country Park was given to the City of Glasgow in 1966 by the Maxwell family and is now managed by the National Trust for Scotland. It is an important haven for wildlife within an urban setting, especially in the White Cart Water neighbourhood. Heron, foxes, bats and woodpeckers are just some of the local residents. Pollok House itself was designed by William Adam in the classical style in the mid eighteenth century. On its walls hang one of the best collections of Spanish art in private hands in Britain with paintings by El Greco and Goya amongst others. Visitors can also see 'below stairs' and visit the café. This is housed in a vast Edwardian kitchen with a high domed ceiling, walls lined with pale green tiles, rows of gleaming copper pans and a 4 metre cast-iron range, complete with a water-driven spit. Before the Trust took over, all this was for a family of three! Self-guided trails lead through Pollok Park from the Countryside Rangers' Centre near to the old stable courtyard. Amongst the many highlights of a walk through the park are the demonstration gardens inside the former walled garden, the wildlife garden, and the various castles which have occupied this site for many centuries. There are excellent riverside walks along the White Cart Water which flows through Cathcart before emerging into the River Clyde.

The Burrell Collection building

The City Chambers, George Square

4 Celtic Football Club Visitor Centre & Museum

Situated at Celtic Park, the Celtic Visitor Centre tells the history of the Celtic Football Club since its beginnings in 1888. Its collections include artefacts, memorabilia, trophies, medals and portraits. There are also guided tours of the stadium, its exhibitions and auditorium. See feature on page 29.

O9 *Celtic Park, Parkhead off the A763.*

P WC ♿ ♨ E AV 🎧 £££

🕐 Daily, excluding match days: 4 tours at 11am, 12noon, 1.45pm and 2.30pm.
Restaurant open Sun only.

Tel 0141 551 4308   www.celticfc.net

5 City Chambers ★

Built to reflect the city's pride as 'Second City of Empire', this impressive nineteenth-century building is home to the headquarters of Glasgow City Council. The interior features pillars and staircases in marble and granite, mosaic floors and lavishly painted ceilings. Though a working building, there are regular public tours.

W3 *George Square, Glasgow city centre.*

♿ FREE

🕐 Mon–Fri, 9am–4.30pm;
guided tours at 10.30am & 2.30pm.
Closed public holidays.

Tel 0141 287 4018
www.glasgow.gov.uk

6 City Sightseeing Glasgow ★

Passengers can view Glasgow from an open-top bus, and listen to multi-lingual commentary, or live commentary by a guide. Tickets are valid all day, allowing people to leave the bus and visit attractions *en route*, then board again for a later tour. Tickets are available from the driver and Tourist Information Centres in the city.

W3 *Tours depart from George Square, City Centre. You can also hop on or off at stops throughout the city.*

♿ £££

🕐 First tour 9.30am, last tour 4.30pm, departing George Square every 15–20 minutes.

Tel 0141 204 0444
www.scotguide.com

CLYDE WALKWAY

With the decline of shipbuilding on the Clyde, the river became pretty quiet. But over the last 20 years that has begun to change. The river banks are being brought back to life. The Clyde Walkway runs in various stages from the Glasgow Tall Ship near the Scottish Exhibition & Conference Centre (SECC) to the Falls of Clyde at Lanark, 64 km upstream. The Council's ambition to reconnect the city with its river is a case of 'work in progress'. There are spectacular, space-age projects like the Science Centre and the 'Armadillo', as the Clyde Auditorium is known, but there are still some sad scenes. Gradually these stretches of past industries are disappearing as more people are lured to live and work here. BBC Scotland is moving from the West End to Pacific Quay on the south bank, while Glasgow Harbour is a new 50-hectare development of offices, shops and flats just downstream from the SECC. And, if all goes to plan, 2009 will see the opening of the new £50 million Riverside Museum beside Glasgow Harbour, designed by the avante-garde Iraqi architect, Zaha Hadid.

The Tall Ship, or *SV Glenlee*, is a three-masted sailing ship launched in 1896 and one of only five such Clyde-built vessels still afloat. Onboard exhibitions detail her past life carrying coal, grain and guano from the four corners of the world. Upstream from here, past the Armadillo, is the Rotunda and the Finnieston Crane. The former is a curious round brick building built in the 1890s to be the northern terminal of a complex of tunnels beneath the Clyde. Foot passengers, horse-drawn carriages and later cars were lowered in lifts to cross under the river. The tunnels were eventually abandoned and the Rotunda is now a restaurant and casino. The Finnieston Crane towers 53 metres above the river and used to hoist whole railway carriages onto waiting ships. It has been silent for many years. The Walkway continues upstream to Anderston Quay, where the *Waverley* – the world's last sea-going paddle steamer – is often moored, and to the Broomielaw. It was here that every summer thousands of Glaswegians once set off on their holidays.

Beyond Victoria Bridge you can follow the Clyde past Glasgow Green to King's Bridge and the King's Haugh where Bonnie Prince Charlie reviewed his troops after their retreat from the south, just a few months before defeat at Culloden in 1746. From here to the Tall Ship is about two miles.

7 Clydebuilt Scottish Maritime Museum

An exhibition charting the development of Glasgow and the Clyde from 1700 to the present day. The story is told through audio-visuals, computer interactives, hands-on displays, video and temporary exhibitions. Visitors can eavesdrop in the shipyard manager's office, see the tools of the trade and walk through all the stages of building a ship.

G11 *Beside Braehead Shopping Centre at J25a (westbound) and J26 (eastbound) off the M8. Follow directions to the 'green' car park.*

P WC & ♿ E AV ££

🕐 Mon–Thur & Sat, 10am–5.30pm; Sun 11am–5pm; Fri, local & school holidays please call for details

Tel 0141 886 1013
www.scottishmaritimemuseum.org

8 College of Piping

Scotland's oldest centre for the teaching of its national instrument, the bagpipes. Founded in 1944, its museum contains a selection of instruments, photographs and memorabilia. Visitors wishing to hear the bagpipes played are welcome.

S6 *Otago Street, west end of Glasgow*

P WC & ♿ E ♿ FREE

🕐 Mon-Fri, 9am-5pm.

Tel 0141 334 3587   www.college-of-piping.co.uk

9 Collins Gallery

A part of the University of Strathclyde, this city centre gallery presents an annual programme of 10 temporary exhibitions. These feature fine and applied art, design and multimedia from both Britain and around the world. Its educational activities are geared for different ages and include workshops, conferences, video, dance and music. Groups are welcome for guided tours.

X3 *Richmond Street, Glasgow city centre. 5 mins walk for Queen Street station.*

FREE & WC ♿ ♿ 🚻 E

🕐 All year, Mon–Fri, 10am–5pm. Sat 12 noon–4pm.

Tel 0141 548 2558
www.strath.ac.uk/collections

10 Crookston Castle

A unique castle, originating in the fourteenth/fifteenth centuries, with a main building surrounded by four corner towers, of which only one survives today and is set within twelfth-century earthworks. It suffered demolition around 1489 while being held by the Stewarts of Darnley. Affords excellent views of south-west Glasgow and in 1931, it was the first property to be gifted to the National Trust for Scotland. Now in the care of Historic Scotland.

H8 *Off Brockburn Road, Pollok, SW of Glasgow city centre*

FREE

🕐 Keys available locally at these times: Apr–Sept, daily, 9.30am–6.30pm. Oct–Mar, Mon–Sat, 9.30am–4.30pm; Sun 2–4.30pm.

Tel 0141 883 9606
www.historic-scotland.gov.uk

11 First City Tour

A classic tour of Glasgow in a 1950s vintage bus. Tours last 1 hour and 20 minutes and take in some of Glasgow's most famous sites. There is live commentary by experienced guides, and the ticket allows passengers to hop on and off to further explore the city and its attractions.

W3 *George Square, Glasgow city centre and points throughout the city.*

♿ £££

🕐 Daily, Mid Mar–Oct, every 15 mins from 9.30am–5.30pm. Nov–Mid Mar, every 30 mins from 9.30am–5.30pm. Tour lasts 1hr 20 mins.

Tel 0141 636 3190   www.firstcitytour.co.uk

12 Fossil Grove

Eleven fossil trees were discovered here in Victoria Park during excavations in 1887. They provide an insight into an ancient forest that grew here, and the landscape of Glasgow 330 million years ago. Protected in a building, there are information displays for visitors.

I11 *Victoria Park, Whiteinch on A814.*

WC & E

🕐 Apr–Sept, daily 12noon–5pm.

Tel 0141 287 2000
www.glasgowmuseums.com

DOWNTOWN

Although Greater Glasgow is a big sprawling city, the centre is relatively small and based on the same grid pattern as New York. The streets may have names rather than numbers and the 'canyon-effect' may be less striking, but downtown Glasgow does feel a little like Manhattan.

This is where most people work and shop – something Glaswegians are inordinately fond of. Having long since dropped the title 'Second City of the Empire', Glasgow has recently promoted itself as 'Britain's premier shopping centre (after London)'.

With its wide streets and well-lit stores, shopping for clothes is certainly more fun here than in many cities, at least when it is not raining. Most shoppers head for what has been dubbed the 'Golden Z' – a pedestrianised area that runs from mid-way down Sauchiehall Street to Argyle Street via the more upmarket Buchanan Street in the middle. Here you can find all the usual suspects among retailers plus a good sprinkling of the more boutique chains like Jigsaw and Hobbs.

At its hub is the Buchanan Galleries, a large complex of some 80 shops next to the Royal Concert Hall. It is based around a flagship branch of John Lewis along with Mango, Gap, Virgin Cosmetics and a very good whisky shop. As shopping malls go it is bright, futuristic and fragrant – having banished Burger King to the top floor. By comparison Argyle Street offers

Princes Square

a more 'bargain basement' experience, possibly having peaked too early. Its Argyle Arcade, built in the Parisian style, was Scotland's first indoor shopping mall when it opened in 1827.

From here Argyle Street runs west straight into Central Station and under a huge railway bridge. Long ago this was dubbed the 'Heilanman's Umbrella' – a reference to all the displaced Highlanders who arrived in the mid nineteenth century looking for work They used to gather here, talk Gaelic and presumably shelter from the rain. To this day, many Glaswegian men appear not to own a brolly.

Sauchiehall Street may not have quite the same retail pulling power as it once had, but it does have a number of points of interest. Its most famous landmark is at No. 217 – the Willow Tea Rooms – whose interior was designed by Charles Rennie Mackintosh and his wife in 1903 (see pages 42 and 58). The nearby McLellan Galleries have been showcasing some of the highlights of the Kelvingrove collection until the restored Museum is reopened in 2006, while further west is the Centre for Contemporary Arts. The CCA offers a cultural mix including dance and theatre, and has a highly rated café-restaurant.

Argyle Street

GLASGOW FOOTBALL

The first Glasgow football club was Queens Park, founded in 1867. A year later the club secretary wrote a letter to Glasgow Thistle FC inviting them to a match lasting two hours with 20 players on each side. From these endearingly amateur roots football developed quickly in Scotland, becoming more and more popular especially in Glasgow.

Celtic F.C., Celtic Park

The letter, together with over 2000 other exhibits, is on display at the Scottish Football Museum at Scotland's national stadium – Hampden Park. The museum's collection of memorabilia traces football's rapid transformation from a hobby into the most popular team game in the world. Visitors can also tour the stadium and even have their footballing skills assessed by a machine that calculates the speed you can kick a ball. Hampden was once the largest stadium in Britain with a capacity of 135,000, a figure now reduced to just 52,000 because of safety reasons.

The exhibition traces the highs and lows of the last 120 years. If one of the defining moments for Scottish fans was hearing that England had won the World Cup, one of the sweetest came just a year later when the Scots beat the English at Wembley in 1967.

Celtic was founded in 1888 by a Roman Catholic priest in an effort to alleviate the poverty of the East End. Meanwhile a team called Rangers that used to play on Glasgow Green had been formed sixteen years earlier. In Scotland the game turned

Rangers F.C., Ibrox

professional in 1893 and a year later, in their first ever meeting, Rangers beat Celtic 3-1. These two clubs, known collectively as the 'Old Firm', dominated Scottish football and have done ever since. In fact so dominant that they may one day join the Premiership League in England.

Between the wars Rangers were almost invincible, winning the old First Division no fewer than 14 times. Then, in the mid 1960s, under their manager Jock Stein, Celtic surged past to become champions at home and in Europe. Their greatest moment probably came in 1967 when the 'Lisbon Lions' became the first ever British Club to win the European Cup when they beat Inter Milan 2-1. Rangers followed five years later beating Moscow Dynamo to win the now defunct Cup Winners' Cup.

While Rangers and Celtic have thrived on their local rivalry, today both teams are thoroughly international, so international that it seems incredible when Celtic won the European Cup in 1967, every player was born and lived within a 35-mile radius of the city centre.

GALLERY OF MODERN ART

Hard though it is to believe, the Gallery of Modern Art, just one block south of George Square, was once the country home of William Cunninghame, one of the wealthiest Tobacco Lords. It was built in 1775 and later became the city's Royal Exchange where commodities like rum, sugar, coal and iron ore were traded for over a hundred years. More recently it has been a telephone exchange and library, until its conversion in 1996 to become one of the top venues for contemporary art in the country.

The handsome neo-classical building almost fills Royal Exchange Square and boasts a towering set of Corinthian columns out front together with a statue of the Duke of Wellington on his horse. For some reason there is almost invariably a large traffic cone perched on the Duke's head.

Inside there are more columns supporting a high barrel-vaulted roof, and above this soars a delightful atrium and skylight. The spacious ground floor makes a wonderful backdrop for the works on display and these could be anything from scrap-metal sculptures to large figurative paintings. In the first- and second-floor galleries above, work from the GoMA's permanent collection are displayed on rotation.

The gallery's stated aim is to make art and contemporary culture accessible to all its visitors, and by and large they achieve this with a fresh, non-élitist approach to modern art.

The collection and rolling programme of exhibitions focus on works created since the 1950s by home-grown and international artists using a wide range of media including sculpture, photography, video and installation art. Artists frequently represented include Beryl Cook, Peter Howson and Andy Goldsworthy. There is a well-stocked shop on the ground floor and a café in the basement.

13 Gallery of Modern Art 🏛

This is the second most visited contemporary art gallery outside London. Nicknamed 'GoMA', its collections are housed in the Royal Exchange building, which was once a tobacco merchant's mansion. Its contains four floors of contemporary paintings, sculpture and installations from around the world. As well as its permanent collections, GoMA hosts regular temporary exhibitions and has an active education programme of workshops, projects and talks.

W3 *Queen Street, Glasgow city centre.*

🚻 ♿ ☕ 🏛 E ♿ FREE

🕐 Mon–Wed & Sat, 10am–5pm;
Thur, 10am–8pm: Fri & Sun, 11am–5pm.
Free guided tours.

Tel 0141 229 1996

www.glasgowmuseums.com

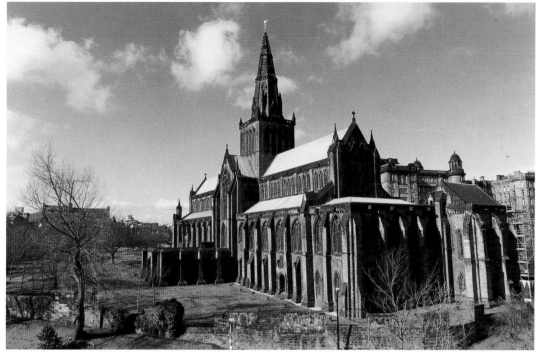

Glasgow Cathedral

14 Glasgow Cathedral

The present cathedral was erected between the thirteenth and fifteenth centuries over the supposed site of the tomb of St Kentigern, who died in 612. The cathedral features a vaulted crypt, carved stones and unique original stone screen. The lower church contains the shrine of St. Mungo, patron saint of Glasgow, who died in 603. The cathedral is in the care of Historic Scotland, and is the only medieval church on the Scottish mainland to have survived the Reformation virtually complete.

Y3 *Cathedral Square, Glasgow city centre.*

& 🏛 E FREE

🕐 Apr–Sept, Mon–Sat, 9.30am–6pm. Sun 1–5pm.
   Oct–Mar, Mon–Sat, 9.30am–4.30pm & Sun 1–4pm.
   Services: Sun 11am & 6.30pm.

Tel 0141 552 6891   www.historic-scotland.gov.uk

15 Glasgow Necropolis   ★

This opulent cemetery adjacent to Glasgow Cathedral was created in the nineteenth century. It is the resting place of many of Glasgow's famous citizens and contains an array of memorials and structures of architectural interest. It is modelled on the Père Lachaise Cemetery in Paris and has excellent views over Glasgow.

Y3 *Adjacent to Glasgow Cathedral, Glasgow city centre.*

P FREE

🕐 Dawn to dusk.

Tel 0141 287 3961

16 Glasgow Police Museum

A museum that tells the story of Britain's oldest police force from 1779-1975. Uniforms, badges, truncheons and medals combine with display boards that illustrate the 200-year history of the Glasgow police. Complementary to the historical displays is the International Police Exhibition, which showcases uniforms and insignia from police forces around the world.

X2 *St Andrew's Square, Glasgow*

WC & E FREE

🕐 Apr–Oct, daily, Mon–Sat 10am–4.30pm,
   Sun 12noon–4.30pm. Nov–Mar, Tues
   10am–4.30pm, Sun 12noon–4.30pm.

Tel 07788 532691

www.policemuseum.org.uk

GLASGOW GREEN AND THE PEOPLE'S PALACE

The city's oldest park was originally an area for grazing animals and washing and bleaching linen, but as the city's population boomed during the nineteenth century this pleasant open space came under increasing threat. Near the heart of old Glasgow, just east of the High Street, the Green has long been used as an assembly point for public protests. These have ranged from the Chartist demonstrations of the 1830s and '40s, to the CND anti-nuclear protests of the 1960s to the recent large gathering of people against the war in Iraq. For centuries the Green was also the venue for the Glasgow Fair; originally a horse market it has now become a general public holiday in July. The Green has a wealth of interesting memorials, many of them fountains. Amongst these are the McLennan Arch at the entrance, the large Doulton Fountain made for the Glasgow International Exhibition in 1888 but sadly recently vandalised, and the Collins Fountain, erected by the publisher Sir William Collins (1817-95) whose temperance attempts to curb Glasgow's addiction to the demon drink earned him the nickname of 'Water Willie'. There is also the James Watt memorial stone commemorating the day in 1765 when the great inventor had his 'eureka' moment: it was while walking across the Green that Watt resolved how his steam engine would work.

The People's Palace at the northern end of the Green opened in 1898 as a folk museum. Recently refurbished, it is still very much 'for the people', in contrast to the more highbrow culture displayed in the city's other galleries and museums. It contains a remarkable and sometimes eclectic collection of items from Glasgow's past. Here you can find out about the 'Steamies' (public laundry houses), enter a prison cell, experience something of going 'Doon the Watter' on a Clyde steamer, or view the banana boots worn by the great Glaswegian comedian Billy Connolly. Other sections refer to trades unionism, political dissent and drinking. Among the more bizarre exhibits is a barrow used by the Glasgow constabulary to wheel drunks home. In all it is a remarkable assembly of social history representing over a thousand years of life in this proud city. To the rear of the museum are the Winter Gardens, an enclosed botanical construction now used as the pleasant cafeteria area for the museum. Just to the east of the People's Palace is the building known as Templeton's Carpet Factory. Built in the Venetian style in the 1890s by architect William Leiper, it has been described as 'the world's finest example of decorative brickwork'. It has a wealth of symbolic representations on its façade and a myriad of architectural details. Templeton carpets were commissioned for the *Queen Mary* liner.

17 Glasgow School of Art ★ ☼

Glasgow School of Art, still a working art school, is Charles Rennie Mackintosh's greatest architectural masterpiece. Guided tours take visitors through various corridors to the Gallery, Mackintosh Room and Library, where they can see his unique interiors and furniture. See the Mackintosh feature on pages 42-47.

V4 *Renfrew Street, Glasgow city centre.*

[WC] ♿ ⌂ E ⊞ ££

🕐 Guided tour times: Apr–Sept, daily, 10.30, 11 & 11.30am, 1.30, 2 & 2.30pm. Oct–Mar, Mon–Fri, 11am & 2pm; Sat 10.30 & 11.30am.

Tel 0141 353 4526
www.gsa.ac.uk

Glasgow School of Art – North Face

GLASGOW SCIENCE CENTRE

While London was building its ill-fated Millennium Dome beside the River Thames, Glasgow was constructing its dazzling new Science Centre on the south bank of the River Clyde. The Centre has its very own flag-pole in the form of the Glasgow Tower that rises over 100 metres above the river. This slender silver tube is shaped like the upturned wing of a plane and is designed to always face into the wind. Visitors are shown how the tower sits on a solitary ball bearing, little more than a foot wide, at its base. A set of small electric motors allows it to rotate 360 degrees.

Provided the wind speed is no more than 40 miles per hour, you can take one of the external glass lifts to the top of the Tower for what is without doubt the best view in town. As the lift travels upwards you gain a real sense of the city's expanding horizons, a theme developed in the 'Past Visions' gallery which explores how Glasgow has changed over the last 300 years. Beside it, the 'Future Visions' gallery reveals some of the hopes, dreams and fears Glaswegians have for their city.

The top of the Glasgow Tower is also a great place to look down and take in the Science Centre itself. From up here it resembles a giant slice of watermelon with a silvery titanium skin. The side facing the river is completely made of glass.

The Science Centre is spread over three floors and has over 300 hands-on exhibits – many of them fully interactive. There are also live science shows that last 30 minutes and cover a wide range of topics – anything from climate change to exploring parts of the human body to what gives fizzy drinks their fizz.

There is also a large planetarium where city dwellers can view the night sky as they may never have seen it before – in perfect darkness. And afterwards you can visit the new IMAX cinema next door where you can watch films in 3-D on a screen that is larger than a 5-a-side football pitch.

18 Glasgow Science Centre 🏛

This millennium project, situated on the River Clyde, is comprised of: an IMAX theatre shows educational films on a huge screen, the Science Mall contains exhibits, hands-on demonstrations, and the Space Theatre's modern planetarium, while the Glasgow Tower, topping 127m high, rotates 360°, offering views of the city and beyond. See feature above.

R3 *Pacific Quay, on south bank of the Clyde.*

🅿 ♿ 🚾 🍷 ✗ 🚮 E 📺 🚏 ♨ 📮 ££

⊕ Science Mall open daily, 10am–6pm. Film & show times vary; check website or telephone for details.

Tel 0141 420 5000   www.gsc.org.uk

Kelvingrove Art Gallery and Museum

Glasgow Cathedral and Cathedral Square

19 Govan Old Church ☦

Located on a historic Christian site, the current building was completed in 1888. The church contains a collection of early medieval carved stones, including Viking 'hogback' tombstones, and the Govan Sarcophagus.

I10 *Govan Road, Glasgow off A8,
90 metres W of Govan underground.*

[AV] ☼ FREE

🕐 Daily Worship 10am, Sun 11am.
Jun–Sep, Wed, Thur & Sat, 1pm–4pm
or by special arrangement.

Tel 0141 440 2466   www.govanold.org.uk

20 Hidden Gardens ❀

A derelict wasteland transformed into contemplative gardens. Designed with a mixture of native and exotic species, the gardens also incorporate a number of artworks. There are numerous themed workshops and events held throughout the year.

L8 *Tramway, Albert Drive, Pollokshields
off the Pollokshaws Road, SW of city centre.*

[P] [WC] [♿] [🍽] [⛱] FREE

🕐 May–Sept, Tue–Sat, 10am–8pm.
Sun, 12 noon–6pm. Oct–Apr, Tue–Sat, 10am–4pm.
Sun 12 noon–4pm. Closed Mon.
Tours of the Gardens, Wed, Jun–Sep, 1pm.

Tel 0141 433 2722
www.thehiddengardens.org.uk

21 House for an Art Lover 🏛 ☀

A 1990s-built house based on a number of competition entry drawings produced by Charles Rennie Mackintosh nearly a century earlier. Visitors can tour a number of rooms, and compare Mackintosh's original designs with the recreated interiors, furniture and fittings. See Mackintosh feature on pages 42-47.

I9 *Bellahouston Park, off Dumbreck Road,
S of Glasgow city centre.*

[P] [WC] [♿] [✗] [♨] E [AV] ☼ [👥] [🎫] ££

🕐 Apr–Sept, Mon–Wed, 10am–4pm;
Thur–Sun, 10am–1pm.
Oct–Mar, Sat–Sun, 10am–1pm.

Tel 0141 353 4770
www.houseforanartlover.co.uk

House for an Art Lover

Drawing Room, The Mackintosh House, Hunterian Art Gallery

22 Hunterian Art Gallery incorporating the Mackintosh House

Housed in a purpose-built building at the University of Glasgow, the Hunterian Art Gallery holds paintings by Rembrandt, Chardin and Stubbs, and Scottish Colourists Fergusson, Peploe, Cadell and Hunter. The Gallery's James McNeill Whistler collection is one of the finest in the world. It also contains the Mackintosh House, which includes a reconstruction of the interiors of Charles Rennie Mackintosh's Glasgow home, making use of original designs and furniture. See feature on Mackintosh on pages 42–47.

R6 *The Art Gallery is on Hillhead Street at the University of Glasgow, west end of Glasgow city centre.*

wc & ☕ ⛪ E ♿ FREE

🕐 Mon–Sat, 9.30am–5pm;
Admission charge to the Mackintosh House; Wed free admission after 2pm.

Tel 0141 330 5431
www.hunterian.gla.ac.uk

23 Hunterian Museum

The Hunterian Museum and Art Gallery is the legacy of Dr William Hunter, a pioneering obstetrician, anatomist and teacher who died in 1783. His substantial private collection formed the basis of Scotland's first public museum in 1807 which now contains over a million items. The collections are split into four nearby locations at the University of Glasgow: the Hunterian Museum, the Zoology Museum, the Anatomy Museum, and the Hunterian Art Gallery incorporating the Mackintosh House. The different museums feature wide-ranging archaeological and ethnographic materials, including one of the world's greatest coin collections. See Hunterian Art Gallery under separate entry.

R6 *The Museum is on University Avenue, at the University of Glasgow, west end of Glasgow city centre.*

wc & ☕ ⛪ E ♿ FREE

🕐 Mon–Sat, 9.30am–5pm

Tel 0141 330 4221
www.hunterian.gla.ac.uk

HUNTERIAN ART GALLERY AND MUSEUM

William Hunter (1717–83) became a student at Glasgow University at the age of 13 where he studied anatomy. He later specialised in obstetrics and helped deliver the children of Queen Charlotte, wife of George III. During his life he amassed a large collection covering zoology, books, coins and works of art which he left to the University. This formed the basis of the Hunterian Museum which opened in 1807 as Scotland's first public museum. The collection has been growing ever since. Within the Art Gallery there are works by Rubens, Pissaro and Rembrandt among others, as well as portraits by the eighteenth-century British artists, Ramsay and Reynolds. There is also an extensive collection of Scottish paintings from the nineteenth and early twentieth centuries including over 200 works by the Glasgow Boys (and Girls) and 100 by the Scottish Colourists. Among the highlights are a set of ten beautiful landscapes of Iona by Peploe and Cadell. But the Hunterian's great claim to fame is its collection of paintings by the great nineteenth-century American artist, James McNeill Whistler. It is particularly strong on his later works and portraits, many of them full length. In all there

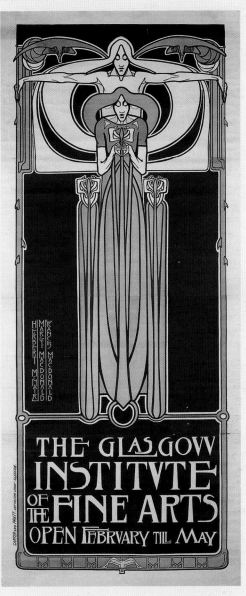

Poster for the Glasgow Institute of Fine Arts, 1896

William Hunter, by Allan Ramsay, 1764

are 80 oils, several hundred drawings and more than 2000 impressions of his prints, making this the largest collection outside his homeland. Whistler's long-handled paintbrushes and other materials are also displayed along with some of his furniture, silver and ceramics to provide a greater insight into the artist.

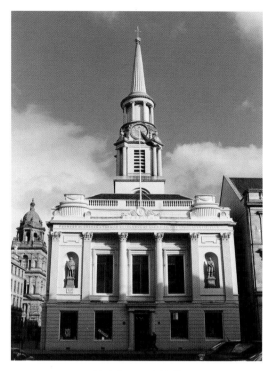

Hutchesons' Hall

24 Hutchesons' Hall 🏛️ 🏛️

One of Glasgow's most elegant buildings, Hutchesons' Hall was built in 1802-5 to a design by David Hamilton. It incorporates statutes from an earlier building of 1641, of George and Thomas Hutcheson who founded Hutchesons' Hospital. It has a permanent multi-media exhibition, Glasgow Style, and a gallery which promotes the work of young Glasgow designers.

X3 *Ingram Street, SE corner of George Square.*

WC ♿ ♨ E FREE

🕐 Gallery and Function Hall: all year round, Mon–Sat, 10am–5pm. Closed 24 Dec–20Jan.

Tel 0141 552 8391   www.nts.org.uk

25 Kelvingrove Art Gallery 🏛️
and Museum

Kelvingrove, with its striking red sandstone façades and grand interiors, is one of Scotland's most popular free attractions. It houses an impressive and hugely varied art collection, silver, ceramics, armour and weaponry, costumes and furniture, plus a large natural history section. Notable artists with works exhibited on the first floor include Rembrandt,

Millet, Van Gogh, Renoir, Sisley, Picasso, Rossetti, McTaggart and the Glasgow Boys. See feature on page 41.

R5 *Kelvingrove, Glasgow.*

🅿️ WC ♿ ♨ ✕ ♨ E AV ♨ ♨ ♨ FREE

🕐 Closed for refurbishment, re-opens in Summer 2006. A selection of exhibits from Kelvingrove can be seen at the McLellan Gallery.

Tel 0141 287 2699   www.glasgowmuseums.com

26 The Lighthouse 🏛️ ☀️

Housed in the former Glasgow Herald Building, the Lighthouse is Scotland's centre for architecture, design and the city, and is home to the Mackintosh Interpretation Centre (an exhibition based on the life and work of Charles Rennie Mackintosh) and a changing programme of exhibitions and events. Other attractions include a children's area and a viewing tower. See also feature on Mackintosh on pages 42-47.

W3 *Mitchell Lane, off Buchanan Street, Glasgow city centre.*

WC ♿ ♨ ✕ ♨ E AV ♨ ♨ £

🕐 Daily, 10.30am–5pm except Tue 11am–5pm & Sun 12 noon–5pm.

Tel 0141 221 6362   www.thelighthouse.co.uk

The Lighthouse

KELVINGROVE ART GALLERY AND MUSEUM

Across the River Kelvin from the University, at the westernmost end of Argyle
Street, stands Glasgow's most popular tourist attraction. The Kelvingrove Museum
and Art Gallery is a colossal piece of municipal architecture in pink sandstone
that opened in 1902. It was built on the proceeds of the highly successful Glasgow
Exhibition of 1888 to house one of the most important civic collections in Europe.
Visitor numbers were over a million a year by the time it closed for a recent major
restoration, making it Britain's most visited museum outside London.

These numbers are set to rise when Kelvingrove re-opens in the summer of
2006 after £27.9 million has been spent on the building. The refurbishment aims
to restore the interior to its Edwardian splendour and, by expanding into the
basement, increase its exhibition space by a third. This will mean that the
number of objects on display will leap from 5000 to just under 8000.

In terms of paintings the collection ranges from Italian and Dutch Old Masters, to French
impressionist and post-impressionist works, to the Glasgow Boys and Scottish Colourists
of the late nineteenth and early twentieth centuries. Highlights include Rembrandt's
'A Man in Armour', Constable's 'Hampstead Heath' and Thomas Faed's 'The Last of the Clan'.
In the vast natural history section you can walk among the dinosaurs, admire Sir Roger
the Elephant or ponder 300 million-year-old marine fossils from the Glasgow area.
The Museum also boasts one of the finest collections of arms and armour in the world
and includes a near-complete set of fifteenth-century field armour, the oldest in existence.
Rather than display everything according to their various disciplines and categories,
the new Kelvingrove is being split into 22 themes ranging from 'Cultural
Survival' to 'Creatures of the Past'. There will also be three new interactive 'Discovery'
centres, covering art, natural history and history & technology, and an audio-visual
'Object Cinema'. Add in a dedicated space for touring exhibitions, a better
shop, a bigger restaurant.... not to mention its much-improved toilets,
and Glasgow's flagship museum should be a winner when it re-opens.

CHARLES RENNIE MACKINTOSH

'Scotland with Style' is how Glasgow likes to portray itself, this being the latest description used to promote the city. Encapsulating that thoroughly Glaswegian sense of 'style', one figure stands out above all others. Working a hundred years ago, Charles Rennie Mackintosh was one of Scotland's greatest architects. But he was more than just an architect, he was a consummate artist.

His building work was almost all completed in and around his home town of Glasgow and wove together many diverse threads from the world of design and decorative arts. He believed passionately that architecture was an art form that brought all the arts together. In his best-loved creations like The Hill House and Glasgow School of Art, his vision took in everything from the overall shape of the building to the tiniest interior detail. His buildings were a mix of bold, confident draughtsmanship coupled with a wonderfully original sense of the aesthetic. Working with his wife Margaret, a talented decorative artist in her own right, he designed the furniture, the wall fittings, the windows, the lights... everything to create a harmonious whole.

Not that he found his talents wholly appreciated at the time, and after a brief moment of glory, he more or less abandoned Glasgow for ever in 1914, having had no new architectural commissions for four years. Only recently has his reputation been restored and Glasgow has been making up for lost time. There is now a trail of Mackintosh properties throughout the city you can visit, including a permanent exhibition at the Lighthouse. Meanwhile his designs have been commercially plundered and reproduced, especially in jewellery, which is sold in every gift shop in town. 'Mockintosh' is now big business, and one wonders what Mackintosh himself would make of it all. Though his work has influenced many architects and designers since, he did not start any great architectural movement. He was a complete one-off – a true original like the city of his birth.

Charles Rennie Mackintosh was born in 1868 in the Townhead area of Glasgow near the Cathedral, the son of a police superintendent and one of 11 children. After leaving school at 16, Mackintosh began studying art and architecture in the evenings at the old Glasgow School of Art while he worked as an apprentice architect during the day-time. The latter was a sober, entirely male profession where people wore high starched collars and three-piece suits. Life as an art student was very different and far more feminine. It was here that he formed a group of like-minded friends known as 'The Four' that included Herbert McNair and the two Macdonald sisters – Frances, and Margaret whom he married in 1900.

It was during these years that he explored the interplay of architecture, painting and decorative arts which was to define his career. He was influenced by all the leading trends of the day from Art Nouveau and Symbolism to the whole Arts and Crafts movement. What made his work unique, however, was the blending in of deep-rooted Scottish traditions. His work was modernist and forward-looking, but it was also firmly grounded in Scotland.

Having joined one of the city's leading architects, Honeyman & Keppie, his big break came in 1896 when his designs were chosen for the new Glasgow School of Art, a project that was finally completed in 1909. In the intervening years he designed schools, churches, private homes and interiors for a string of up-market tea-rooms. His fall from prominence, accompanied perhaps by depression and drinking, took him and Margaret to Suffolk in 1914, and then to France in the 1920s. Having given up architecture completely he devoted his remaining years to painting watercolour landscapes of extraordinary quality before dying aged 60 in 1928.

Glasgow School of Art front entrance

Mackintosh's Masterwork

By common consent, the Glasgow School of Art was the greatest architectural triumph of Charles Rennie Mackintosh's career. But it was a triumph in two parts, because the governors of the school could only afford the first part of Mackintosh's design. It was over ten years later, in 1907, before he was commissioned to build the west wing and complete the job. By then he was approaching 40, a fully mature architect at the height of his powers, and yet for reasons that seem extraordinary now, the second phase of the Art School was to be his last real building project. Apart from various tea room interiors and a small domestic job in England, his architectural days were all but over.

During his time as a student at the old School of Art, he got to know Francis Newbery, the head of the School; he and his wife Jessie, were to become life-long friends. The old School of Art had been looking to move out of its stuffy, gas-lit studios on Sauchiehall Street for some

Glasgow School of Art clock

time. Finally a suitable site was found and when enough money was raised eleven architects were invited to submit to a competition. Knowing Newbery cannot have hindered Mackintosh's chances, but the design he came up was superb, being bold and modern, yet softened by the playful use of more traditional Scots imagery. The front of the building on Renfrew Street has been likened to two art factories framing a lovable old castle in the middle. In 1985, the American architect, Robert Venturi described this façade as 'comparable in scale and majesty to Michelangelo'. On either side of the central core giant windows flood the studios behind with daylight. Before entering, look at the carved stone portal above the entrance in which two women kneel facing a stylised rose bush. The flower was a constant motif in the designs of Mackintosh and his wife Margaret. Of all the interiors, the library is the most striking. A tall room panelled in dark wood with wooden pillars supporting a narrow gallery. The effect has been likened to a forest clearing with daylight filtering in through elongated windows that stretch up to the ceiling.

Scotland Street School

Mackintosh's Architecture

In 1895, the year before submitting plans for the Glasgow School of Art, Mackintosh designed the Martyrs' School. Now used by the Museums Conservation department, the interior has remained pretty much unchanged, showing what a conventional co-ed school would have felt like a hundred years ago. He went on to design the Scotland Street School in 1903. The intervening years had given him the confidence to develop his own unique style of architecture. The front of the building is flanked by two spectacular towers in curved glass that housed the stair wells – one for the boys and one for the girls. Both are topped with conical slate roofs to resemble castle turrets. Any visitor should climb to the top to see the vast cookery room with its 7 metre dresser and cabinet designed by Mackintosh, and then take in the magnificent views north across Glasgow. Having designed Windyhill, a private home at Kilmacolm in Renfrewshire in 1899, Mackintosh was commissioned to draw up plans for a second private dwelling four years later. The Hill House in Helensburgh, built for the Glasgow publisher

Windyhill, Kilmacolm

Perhaps there were not enough patrons in Glasgow with the wealth and vision to employ Mackintosh at the time, but he never designed another private home there after The Hill House. Maybe he was in the wrong place at the wrong time, for his ideas were more in tune with the prevailing architectural currents in central Europe. In 1901 he and his wife Margaret were invited to Vienna to take part in an exhibition. While there they entered a competition for a German magazine to design a House for an Art Lover in which the interior and exterior had to be a coherent work of art. Although they didn't win, the plans were published by the competition sponsors a year later. For many years these sketches remained just a curiosity, something only for real Mackintosh aficionados. All that changed in 1996, when after seven years in the making, the House for an Art Lover opened in Bellahouston Park based on a faithful interpretation of Mackintosh's original designs. Today it is a centre for postgraduate students at Glasgow School of Art, but a number of the rooms are open to the public including the music room whose intense symbolism is balanced

The Hill House, Helensburgh

Walter Blackie, is regarded as one of his finest achievements. It is now cared for by the National Trust for Scotland and open to the public.

On the outside The Hill House is a substantial family home with more than a nod to the Scots 'baronial' style with its roughcast walls and central pepper-pot turret. But on entering, the further in you go into the deep recesses of the house the more different it becomes. Just off the main hall is the library or study where Walter Blackie received his visitors. With its stained wood, the décor is dark, sombre and traditional, in complete contrast to the cool elegance and minimalism of the master bedroom, with its creamy walls and white lacquered furnishings. The Hill House has two sides to it, one masculine, strong, business-like and somewhat conservative, the other sensual, feminine and modernist.

For the main rooms of the house, the Blackies' bedroom, the library, the drawing room and hallways, Mackintosh had complete control. The decoration of the walls, the carpets, the chairs, clocks and cabinets were all designed or chosen by him. And everywhere are little flourishes to catch the eye, from inlaid fragments of coloured glass and ceramics to wall stencils and fittings. The attention to detail and the level of thought that went into the layout of the rooms and the positioning of the furniture is extraordinary.

Drawing Room, The Mackintosh House

by an invigorating sense of space and light. Its excellent ground-floor café is another draw.

Meanwhile back in the West End at the Hunterian Art Gallery is the Mackintosh House. Like the House for an Art Lover, this too is an interpretation and an attempt to make amends for the fact that the few homes Mackintosh designed in Glasgow itself no longer exist.

But the display is not about external architecture so much as interior design. It is an attempt to reproduce the space he and his wife lived in, a space meticulously designed by the two of them together. The scene is based on contemporary photographs of the couple's home and uses their own original artwork and furniture. They lived in a flat in Mains Street, which they did up after their marriage in 1900, and later moved to Florentine Terrace taking all their fittings with them. On entering the Mackintosh House, note the ways used to make the narrow hall feel wider, including the large Art Nouveau mirror with its peacock tails and leaping fish designed by Margaret and her sister Frances. Off the hall lies a small, dark dining room, where the furnishings have all been carefully designed to fit. The only things missing are the Mackintosh candlesticks and silverware that would once have graced the table. Upstairs through a door decorated with pink glass tears, the mood could not be more different. The studio and the drawing room beyond are painted white to show off their uncluttered sense of space. Here and there a few beautifully crafted pieces of furniture in black or thick white lacquer are carefully placed to enhance the effect.

Willow Tea Rooms, Sauchiehall Street

The Mackintosh Tea Rooms

Catherine Cranston was the doyenne of Glasgow tea rooms. She was a woman with avant-garde tastes who became Mackintosh's most faithful patron. Tea rooms filled a social need, a place for men to lunch, smoke and play billiards without the temptations of drink. More importantly they were somewhere for respectable women to meet in comfort and safety. At the time women in public without men tended to be taken for servants or prostitutes.

After a couple of small commissions from Cranston, the Mackintoshes were given their first full interior to design in 1900. This was the Ladies Luncheon Room in Ingram Street where Charles and Margaret used leaded glass panels in pale green, black and white to divide the different seating areas. By the windows were banquettes facing black tall-backed chairs, while the couple's artwork in the form of two giant, curving panels hung on opposite walls.

The grandest of Catherine Cranston's restaurants is the Willow Tea Rooms on Sauchiehall Street. The phrase 'tea rooms', however, doesn't really do justice to what was more like a luxury club spread over two floors with separate rooms for men and ladies to dine, smoke and sip tea. Its modern-day equivalent would be the most stylish of style bars, designed by the most contemporary, cutting-edge

Cuckoo Flower, Chiddingstone, 1910

Mackintosh As Artist

After completing the Art School in 1908, Mackintosh barely worked again in his home town. One of his few commissions came from the faithful Miss Cranston to design a couple of rooms on Ingram Street in 1911. On the outbreak of the First World War, he and Margaret went to Suffolk for an extended painting holiday. In that first year he produced a large number of elegant botanical sketches. He had always been interested in flowers and used them constantly in his textiles and furnishings. Most popular of all was a stylised rose stencilled onto wall hangings, drapes and linen chair-backs. Mackintosh and his wife continued to design textiles often with bold, geometric patterns when they moved to London half way through the war. He was also commissioned to convert a small terraced house in Derngate, Northampton and to design a basement tearooms (the 'Dug-Out') for Miss Cranston's Willow Tea Rooms. This was his last work in Glasgow and an end of his architectural career.

The couple left London in 1923 and moved to the south of France. They stayed in a succession of inexpensive hotels before ending up at Port-Vendres on the edge of the Pyrenees. Here Mackintosh painted a series of remarkably observed watercolour landscapes before returning to London in 1927. He died the following year of cancer, aged 60.

designer, though with one crucial difference of course; Miss Cranston's establishments were completely alcohol free.

Only the first floor remains with a tea gallery at the back and the Room de Luxe overlooking Sauchiehall Street at the front. They were extensively restored in 1983 by Geoffrey Wimpenny, of Keppie Henderson, the same architectural firm Mackintosh had worked for over a century before. Some things have been lost, like the chandelier with its rose-coloured glass baubles, or else removed for safe-keeping, like the beautifully decorated glazed doors that separated the Room de Luxe from the outside world (replica doors are now in use). Even so there remains a sense of magic and you can still almost picture the scene whereby groups of Glaswegian ladies would gather here for lunch, their genteel gossip reverberating off the walls. The walls were clad in grey silk stitched with beads, above which hung mirrored panes of glass separated by thin white vertical lines. The banquettes and chair covers are upholstered in their original purple velvet while the chairs themselves are painted silver.

La Rue du Soleil, France, 1926

Martyrs' School

27 Martyrs' School ★ ▦

Originally designed by architect Charles Rennie Mackintosh and opened in 1897 as a primary school. It was refurbished in 1999 and is now used as offices by Glasgow Museums' staff. It is open to the public by appointment only. Martyrs' School is one of Mackintosh's early works, and while its plan is similar to other board schools of its time, it contains many early examples of what later developed into the architect's internationally recognised style. Worth a look are the Art Nouveau motifs around the entrance and, in particular, the distinctive roof trusses over the stair. See also feature on Mackintosh on pages 42-47.

Y4 *Parson Street, Glasgow city centre. Parking available at Glasgow Cathedral.*

P ⬛ ♿ ⛪ E ▣ FREE

🕐 Daily, Mon–Thur & Sat, 10am–5pm.
Fri & Sun, 11am–5pm.
Closed 25, 26 & 31 Dec pm, 1 & 2 Jan.
To book a visit call St Mungo Museum on Tel 0141 553 2557.

Tel 0141 553 2557
www.glasgowmuseums.com

28 McLellan Galleries 🏛

The McLellan Galleries first opened in 1854 to house the private collection of Glasgow industrialist and coach builder Archibald McLellan. The building was damaged by fire in the 1980s, but extensively restored and reopened in 1990 as a high quality venue for travelling art exhibitions and other prestigious events.

V4 *Sauchiehall Street, Glasgow city centre.*

⬛ ♿ ⬛ ⛪ E ▣ FREE

🕐 All year, Mon-Thu & Sat, 10am-5pm.
Fri & Sun, 11am-5pm.

Tel 0141 565 4137
www.glasgowmuseums.com

29 Mercat Glasgow ★

Guided walking tours of Glasgow lasting approximately 90 minutes. Separate themes of 'Horror' and 'History ' are offered, but should be booked in advance.

W3 *Tours start in the city centre.*

🚶 £££

🕐 Telephone for details of tour times and to book

Tel 0141 586 5378
www.mercat-glasgow.co.uk

30 Mitchell Library 🏛

The Mitchell Library is one of the largest public reference libraries in Europe, and a resource centre for Glasgow and the wider community. Its collections contain many exceptional items, including rare books and manuscripts dating back to the twelfth century. Other notable collections include the world's largest Robert Burns Collection, the Glasgow Collection, the Family History Collection and a wealth of music, maps, literature, law, newspapers and periodicals. You do not have to be a library member or a resident to use its services.

T4 *Located at Charing Cross, Glasgow city centre.*

⬛ ⬛ ⛪ ▣ FREE

🕐 All year, Mon–Thur 9am–8pm.
Fri–Sat, 9am–5pm.

Tel 0141 287 2999
www.glasgow.gov.uk

MERCHANT CITY

Glasgow's Merchant City is a compact grid of streets framed by George Square to the north and the old High Street to the east. Once full of derelict warehouses, the area has been likened to Dublin's Temple Bar and, at a stretch, to the original Greenwich Village in New York. For years no-one really knew what to do with all these large empty buildings and even if they had none of them had the money to do it. This was just as well, because the whole area could have gone the same way as much of post-war Glasgow and been bulldozed into history. Rows of 1960s office blocks, apartments and shops would have filled the void and the Merchant City would never have existed. Luckily this is not what happened, because there are some spectacular buildings, particularly the old City Halls, which are slowly being brought back to life. A prime example is the Corinthian bar and restaurant on Ingram street, that began life as the grand nineteenth-century headquarters of the Union Bank of Scotland. It lay abandoned and was only rescued in the 1990s. Seeing the huge, stunning cupola in the main bar today, it is hard to believe that this was hidden for 40 years beneath a suspended ceiling.
South of Ingram Street is Virginia Street whose name recalls the great eighteenth-century Tobacco barons. Half-way down, the Virginia Galleries was the site of the original Tobacco Exchange, while a block away on Miller Street there is the 'Tobacco Merchant's House' at No.42. Built in 1775 and recently restored it is the oldest house in the Merchant City.
On Glassford Street, The Trades Hall was built by Robert Adam at the end of the eighteenth-century, where 14 different guilds from coopers to bonnetmakers could meet. It is the oldest secular building in Glasgow and is still used by the city's Trades House, a charitable body. It is now open to the public who can come and admire the Grand Hall lined with Belgian silk tapestries.
Back on Ingram Street another former bank has been turned into the Italian Centre, home of Britain's first Versace store, while further on is St David's Church where David Dale, the man famous for New Lanark (see page 78), is buried. A few blocks south of here was once swarming with wholesalers buying flowers, fruit, cheese and meat in the various indoor markets. These beautiful buildings are gradually being converted into restaurants, clubs and shops and there is a real buzz about the place, especially on Friday and Saturday nights. The old Cheesemarket is now a huge bar and restaurant. In the 1960s it was nearly flattened to make way for a supermarket.

The Italian Centre, Merchant City

THE MUSEUM OF TRANSPORT

Glasgow was 'Second City of the Empire' not just because it dominated world shipbuilding for much of the late nineteenth and early twentieth centuries. For a start more railway carriages were built here than anywhere else outside the USA and there was also a sizeable car industry nearby for many years. In short this was a city of transport, and one that obviously deserves its very own Transport Museum.

The Museum is housed in Kelvin Hall – a massive red-brick affair that is also home to an indoor running track and sports complex. The building which looks out onto the murky waters of the River Kelvin was once an Exhibition Hall and before that, a circus. There is everything here from the world's oldest surviving pedal bicycle to a Concorde jet engine. Public transport is well represented with horse-drawn carriages, trams, railway locomotives and buses, and there is a great collection of sports cars and motorbikes.

But one of the most eye-catching exhibits is a truck from Pakistan, every inch as brightly painted as a psychedelic album cover from the 1960s. Beyond is an old caravan from the Faslane Peace Camp that was part of the long-running protest against a Trident nuclear submarine base near Helensburgh. And nearby, in complete contrast, stands a dark, gleaming

Rolls Royce Phantom that used to whisk the Lord Provost around town. There is certainly plenty of social history on display, such as the lorry that used to tour the city in war-time giving bake-a-cake cookery demonstrations to promote thrift and food hygiene. Next to the Spitfire that guards the entrance, a whole city street from the 1930s has been recreated. Along with the parked vintage cars, there is an underground, a pub and a cinema showing archive footage of Glaswegians heading 'doon the watter' for their annual holiday on the 'Costa del Clyde'. Meanwhile shipping is given a whole room with 250 model ships, some so heavy it takes six people to lift them.

31 Museum of Transport 🏛

Cars, trains, trams, bicycles, motor bikes, buses and boats are all on display at this museum devoted to the history of transport. Prominent features include a reconstruction of a 1938 Glasgow street, a car showroom and a railway station with a display of Scottish locomotives. See feature above.

R5 *Bunhouse Road, west side of Kelvingrove Park, Glasgow.*

WC ♿ 🍴 ♿ E AV £ FREE

🕐 Mon–Thur & Sat 10am–5pm;
Fri & Sun, 11am–5pm.
Closed 25, 26 Dec & 31 Dec (pm) & 1, 2 January.

Tel 0141 287 2720
www.glasgowmuseums.com

Pollok House

32 National Piping Centre Museum

A centre that promotes the study and history of the bagpipes in Scotland. In addition to the piping school, there is also a museum and interpretation centre which contains an authoritative collection of instruments and artefacts related to piping. There is also an audio-visual display and commentary in five languages.

W4 *McPhater Street, Glasgow City Centre.*

WC & ☕ 🏛 E AV £ £

🕐 All year, Mon–Fri, 9am–4.30pm.

Tel 0141 353 0220   www.thepipingcentre.co.uk

33 People's Palace

Built on Glasgow Green and opened in 1898, the People's Palace tells the local and social history of the city of Glasgow from 1750; lying adjacent is a glasshouse-style building containing the Winter Gardens with a collection of exotic tropical plants. See feature on page 32.

Y1 *Glasgow Green, E of city centre on A749 or A730.*

P WC & ☕ 🏛 E AV 🪑 FREE

🕐 All year, Mon–Thur & Sat, 10am–5pm;
Fri & Sun, 11am–5pm.
Closed 25, 26 Dec & 31 Dec (pm) & 1, 2 Jan.

Tel 0141 271 2951   www.glasgow.gov.uk

34 Pollok House & Country Park

This fine example of a Georgian house, built by the Maxwell family in 1750, who lived on the site for 700 years, contains a collection of paintings, silver and ceramics. At weekends visitors can see a reconstruction of the way the house might have been run at the turn of the last century. It is set in the centre of Pollok Country Park, also home of the Burrell Collection. See feature on page 24.

I7 *Pollok Country Park, three miles S of Glasgow, off M77 at J1; follow signs for adjacent Burrell Collection.*

P & ☕ ✕ 🏛 E 🪑 🧗 £ ££

🕐 House; Daily, 10am–5pm. Closed 25, 26 Dec & 1, 2 Jan. Country Park; free access.

Tel 0141 616 6410   www.nts.org.uk

35 Pride O' the Clyde ★

A 'waterbus' service that runs between the Braehead Shopping Centre, and the Central Railway Station bridge on the River Clyde. Its scheduled departures pass by the sights and ships of the Clyde, and enable distinctive views of Glasgow from the water. Journeys last approximately half an hour each way. The boat has indoor and outdoor seating and serves refreshments.

V2 *Departs from the bottom of Jamaica Street, under Central Station Bridge and the Braehead Shopping Centre.*

WC ♨ ♿ ££

🕐 Open all year, daily.
Departures from 10am–6.15pm.
Check website or telephone for details.

Tel 07711 250969
www.clydewaterbusservices.co.uk

36 Provand's Lordship 🏰

Glasgow's oldest house. Bishop Muirhead built Provand's Lordship as part of St Nicholas' Hospital in 1471. Since then it has been a manse, an alehouse and sweetshop. It is Glasgow's only medieval house and contains a collection of historic Scottish furniture. Behind the house is the St Nicholas Garden, designed in 1995, this medicinal herb garden is a haven of peace and tranquillity.

Y3 *Castle Street, Glasgow city centre. Parking in Glasgow Cathedral car park.*

♨ 🏛 FREE

🕐 All year, Mon-Thur & Sat 10am-5pm.
Fri & Sun, 11am-5pm.
Closed 25, 26 & 31 Dec(pm) & 1, 2 Jan.

Tel 0141 552 8819   www.glasgowmuseums.com

37 Queen's Cross Church ✞ ☸

A galleried, single-aisled church designed by Charles Rennie Mackintosh in the late nineteenth century. Features of particular interest include its stained glass and carving on wood and stonework. It is now the headquarters of the CRM Society.
See also Mackintosh feature on pages 42-47.

L11 *Garscube Road, half a mile W of Glasgow city centre.*

WC ♿ ♨ 🏛 E ⊞ £

🕐 Mon–Fri, 10am–5pm; Sun 2–5pm.
Last admission 4.30pm. Closed Sat & local holidays, Christmas to New Year inclusive.
Disabled access by prior arrangement.

Tel 0141 946 6600   www.crmsociety.com

38 Rangers Football Club Visitor Centre ★

A tour of Ibrox Stadium, including behind the scenes access to the Dressing, Trophy and Press Rooms. There are also interactive features and an audio visual display telling the story of the Rangers Football Club. Tours last approximately an hour and a half. See also feature on page 29.

J9 *Ibrox Stadium, W of the city centre off the A8*

P WC 🏛 AV ⊞ £££

🕐 Tours, Thu & Fri, 11am, 12.30pm & 2.30pm.
Sun 10.30am. Times are subject to change due to fixture list. Booking advisable.

Tel 0870 600 1972   www.rangers.co.uk

39 Royal Highland Fusiliers Museum

A museum that records the military history of the regiment from its origins to the present. Displays include information panels, cased artefacts and uniforms, weaponry, documents and memorabilia.

U4 *Charing Cross end of Sauchiehall Street, Glasgow city centre.*

WC ♿ 🏛 E FREE

🕐 All year, Mon–Fri 9am–5pm.
Closed Public Holidays.

Tel 0141 332 0961   www.rhf.org.uk

40 Ruchill Church Hall ✞ ☸

Originally a mission hall, it was designed by the architect Charles Rennie Mackintosh in 1899. Still in active use by the present congregation, the hall accepts visitors interested in Mackintosh's work, and provides refreshments. See Mackintosh feature on pages 42-47.

K12 *Shakespeare Street, Glasgow city centre.*

♨ FREE

🕐 Sep-Jun, Mon-Fri, 11am-3pm.
Closed July, Aug & 22 Dec-3 Jan inclusive.
Opening times are subject to change.

Tel 0141 946 6600   www.crmsociety.com

Queen's Cross Church

Scotland Street School

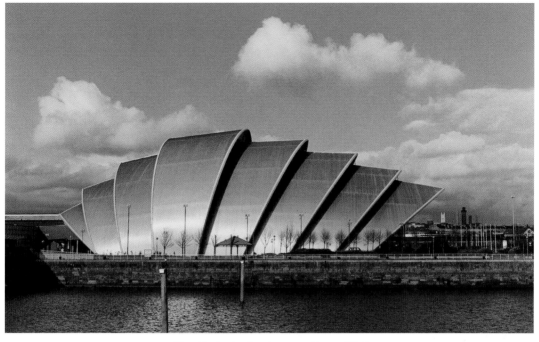

The Clyde Auditorium, or 'Armadillo'

41 Scotland Street School Museum

Glasgow-style stone carving and twin leaded towers feature prominently on this Charles Rennie Mackintosh-designed building. Now a museum dedicated to the history of education, displays include classrooms from different eras, a cookery room and changing exhibitions. See Mackintosh feature on pages 42–47.

T1 *One mile S of city centre opposite Shields Road underground station.*

WC ⓒ ☕ 🏛 E AV FREE

🕐 Mon–Thur & Sat, 10am–5pm;
Fri & Sun, 11am–5pm.
Closed 25, 26 Dec & 1,2 Jan.

Tel 0141 287 0500   www.glasgowmuseums.com

42 Scottish Exhibition & Conference Centre (SECC)   ★

Glasgow's largest events venue. The SECC hosts many concerts, shows, sporting events and exhibitions throughout the year. Contact by phone or online for information on current attractions. Its distinctive Clyde Auditorium is known locally as 'The Armadillo', and it lies just a few minutes' walk over Bell's Bridge on the River Clyde from the equally modern architecture of the Glasgow Science Centre building.

R3 *Off J19 of the M8 near Glasgow city centre.*

P WC ⓒ ☕ ✗ 🏛 ♿

🕐 Telephone or check the website for details and times of events and charges.

General Enquiries Tel 0141 248 3000
Box Office Tel 0870 040 4000   www.secc.co.uk

43 Scottish Football Museum   ★ 🏛

Scotland's football heritage is showcased here at Hampden, Scotland's national football stadium. The museum houses over 2500 exhibits in 14 themed galleries, and the collections include many early and valuable relics of Scotland's footballing past. There is also a separate stadium tour which explores Hampden from the player's view, from the dressing room through to the royal box.

L7 *Hampden Park Football Ground, off the A728 Aikenhead Road, three miles W of Glasgow city centre.*

P WC ⓒ ☕ 🏛 E ♿ ££

🕐 All year, Mon–Sat, 10am–5pm,
Sunday 11am–5pm. Subject to events.

Tel 0141 616 6100
www.scottishfootballmuseum.org.uk

44 Seaforce Power Boats ★

Based at the Tall Ship, Glasgow Harbour, Seaforce provides powerboat rides through Glasgow on the river Clyde. Its longer trips also include a journey to the Clyde Estuary, and wildlife tours. Booking recommended.

Q4 *Glasgow Harbour, follow signs for the Tall Ship.*

P WC 🚻 ⛲ 🏕 ££

🕐 Open all year, daily, 11am–sunset.

Tel 0141 221 1070   www.seaforce.co.uk

45 Sharmanka Kinetic Gallery 🏛

A collection of mechanical sculptures, made by sculptor-mechanic Eduard Bersudsky from hundreds of tiny carved figures and pieces of old scrap. The pieces are choreographed to move to music and synchronised lighting. Sharmanka is Russian for 'hurdy-gurdy' or barrel organ. Full performances last 50 minutes and family matinées for 45 minutes. Book in advance by telephone or e-mail.

X2 *King Street, Merchant City, Glasgow city centre. Disabled access via 109 Trongate.*

♿ ⛲ AV ££

🕐 Full performances: Thur & Sun, 7pm; Children's matinee: Sun, 3pm. Performances can be given at other times for individuals and small groups, please telephone for details.

Tel 0141 552 7080   www.sharmanka.co.uk

46 St Mungo Museum 🏛
of Religious Life and Art

A museum and gallery focusing on different religious faiths in Scotland and throughout the world. Visitors can see a diverse collection of exhibits including Salvador Dali's famous painting 'Christ of St John of the Cross', and wander round the unique Zen garden, symbolising the harmony between people and nature.

Y3 *Castle Street, beside Glasgow Cathedral, Glasgow city centre. Parking in Cathedral car park.*

P WC ♿ 🚻 ⛲ E AV ⛲ 🎫 FREE

🕐 All year, Mon–Thur & Sat, 10am–5pm; Fri & Sun, 11am–5pm. Closed 25,26 & 31 Dec (pm) & 1, 2 Jan.

Tel 0141 553 2557   www.glasgowmuseums.com

47 Tall Ship at Glasgow Harbour ★

Built in 1896, the s. v. *Glenlee* is one of the five last remaining Clyde-built sailing ships still afloat. Recently restored she now houses an exhibition

using interactives describing what life was like on board the ship, where she sailed and the cargoes she carried. A programme of events runs throughout the year.

Q4 *Next to Glasgow SECC, J19 off M8 onto A814, follow signs.*

P WC ♿ ✕ 🚻 E AV 🏕 ⛲ 🎫 ££

🕐 Mar–Oct, daily, 10am–5pm. Nov–Feb, daily, 11am–4pm. Groups telephone for details.

Tel 0141 222 2513   www.thetallship.com

48 Tenement House 🏆 🏛

A typical lower middle class Glasgow tenement flat of the late nineteenth century, consisting of four rooms and retaining most of its original features. The furniture, furnishings and personal belongings of Miss Agnes Toward, who lived in the apartment for over 50 years, present an authentic picture of domestic life at the beginning of the twentieth century. A ground-floor reception flat contains an exhibition on tenement living and the history of tenements in Glasgow.

U5 *Buccleuch Street, near Glasgow School of Art, Glasgow city centre.*

E ££

🕐 Mar–Oct, daily, 1–5pm (last admission 4.30pm). Groups by appointment, weekday mornings only.

Tel 0141 333 0183   www.nts.org.uk

49 Tollcross Park 🐇 🌳 ❀
& Children's Farm

Tollcross Park is famous for its Rose Garden, which hosts the International Rose Trials each year and is at its best in July and August. The Winter Gardens have a nineteenth-century glasshouse, which has recently been restored. The newly added Secret Garden is a sensory area for quiet contemplation. A children's play farm contains horses, ponies, sheep, cattle and rabbits. The visitor centre features interactive displays on nature and the cycle of life.

P8 *Wellshot Road, off the A89 or A74, three miles E of Glasgow city centre.*

 P WC ♿ 🚻 AV 🏕 👫 FREE

🕐 Park, all year, dawn to dusk. Visitor Centre, 10.30am–4pm.

Ranger Service Tel 0141 552 1142
www.glasgow.gov.uk

ALEXANDER 'GREEK' THOMSON

Alexander 'Greek' Thomson was one of the greatest architects of his day. He created some of the finest Victorian buildings in Glasgow and was highly regarded by his peers. But sandwiched between the great Georgian architect, Robert Adam in the eighteenth century and Charles Rennie Mackintosh at the start of the twentieth, his reputation has suffered from neglect. In fact in the 1960s and 1970s some of his buildings were bulldozed into history by Glasgow City Council in the drive for urban renewal.

Thomson was born in 1817 into a huge family as the 17th child of a devout Presbyterian minister. From the age of 12 he worked in a lawyer's office where he was spotted by Robert Foote, a Glasgow architect who took him on as an apprentice. While studying classical buildings during his apprenticeship, he formed the belief that the style of Ancient Greece could be the basis of modern architecture. Nowhere embodied this belief better than **Holmwood House** – the Southside villa he built for James Couper in 1857.

Couper owned a paper mill and wanted a substantial family house to reflect his status. Thomson carefully positioned the house facing to take full advantage of its position overlooking mature trees and sweeping lawns that slope down to the White Cart River. In the distance, 20 miles north, the Campsie Hills are clearly visible from the first floor. While the design is classical, many of the materials were modern, particularly the plate glass used in a huge bow window on the left. This stands behind an imposing semi-circle of columns and by hiding the wooden window frame the effect is to play up the stonework and make the house appear bigger than it actually is. Writing about Holmwood in 1888, fellow architect Thomas Gildard declared that 'If architecture be poetry in stone and lime... this exquisite little gem, at once classic and picturesque, is as complete, self-contained and polished as a sonnet.'

After various owners and a long period as a primary school, Holmwood was almost sold to a developer who planned to build 93 flats and houses in the grounds. It was saved by the National Trust for Scotland in 1994, who began to restore the interior to its former glory and reveal the wealth of Greek and Egyptian imagery on the walls and in the plasterwork.

Right in the centre of Glasgow is one of Thomson's most famous buildings – the St Vincent Street Church, built in 1859. Looking like a Greek temple with a magnificent set of Ionic columns out front and blackened with grime, it squats amidst the hi-rise office blocks, the only one of his churches to survive being burnt, bulldozed by developers or bombed by the Luftwaffe.

Grosvenor Building (1859), Gordon Street, by Greek Thomson

50 Trades Hall of Glasgow ★

The Trades Hall is the historic home of Glasgow's 'Incorporated Crafts and the Trades House', which dates back to 1605 when the body was established to regulate and train trade and craftsmen. The Trades Hall building was commissioned in 1791 and designed by Robert Adam, and is the only major work by Adam surviving in the city today. The Trades House, now a charitable organisation, still meets in the building. Visitors can learn the history of the building and the role of craftsmen and tradesmen in the making and shaping of Glasgow through an audio tour and interactive exhibition.

W3 *Glassford Street, Glasgow city centre.*

WC ♿ 🦮 🏛 E AV ££

🕐 All year. Apr–Oct, Mon–Fri, 10am–5pm, Sat, 10am–2pm. Sun, 12 noon–5pm.
Nov–Mar, Sun, 12 noon–5pm.
Last admission 1 hour before closing.

Tel 0141 552 2418
www.tradeshallglasgow.co.uk

51 University of Glasgow Visitor Centre 🏛

The award-winning visitor centre houses displays and interactive presentations on the history of the University along with information on current events and activities on the campus. A visit to the tower with its camera obscura, gives an alternative view of the University. See also the Hunterian Museum and Hunterian Art Gallery on page 38.

S6 *University Avenue, in the west end of Glasgow.*

WC ♿ 🦮 🏛 E FREE

🕐 Open all year, Mon–Sat, 9.30am–5pm. Sun, 2–5pm. Trips up the tower at 2pm, booking in advance recommended. Check website for details of exhibitions.

Tel 0141 330 5511   www.gla.ac.uk

52 Walkabout Tours ★

Walkabout Tours allow you to take in the history of the city centre at your own pace. Audio sets are available for hire from the Tourist Information Centre in George Square.

During the audio-guided tour you are led to different venues as actors recount the fascinating stories and tales of intrigue of Glasgow's past.

W3 *Main Tourist Information Centre, George Square, city centre.*

🦮 🏛 ££

🕐 All year round.
Tours last 1–3 hours depending on which sites are visited.

Tel 0141 243 2437

53 Waverley Excursions ★

Enjoy a traditional sail on *The Waverley*, an ocean-going paddle steamer, or its sister ship *The Balmoral*. The ships offer day, afternoon and evening cruises round the waters of the Firth of Clyde, including stop-offs at Dunoon and Rothesay on the Isle of Bute, as well as other routes and destinations. Both vessels are equipped with bars, restaurants and heated observation lounges.

T2 *Cruises depart from various ports including Glasgow (Andersons Quay), Dunoon & Rothesay.*

P WC ♿ 🦮 🏛 🚶 ⬛ £££

🕐 Timetable runs from Easter to October. Check website or Tourist Information Offices for tickets and routes.

Tel 0845 130 4647
www.waverleyexcursions.co.uk

54 Willow Tea Rooms ★ ⬚

The interior for this tea room was initially styled by Charles Rennie Mackintosh for Miss Kate Cranston in 1903. The Room de Luxe on the first floor of the building has been restored and is still a tea room open to the public. Mackintosh also remodelled the façade, creating the unique room-wide window.
See Mackintosh feature on pages 42–47.

V4 *Above Hendersons, 217 Sauchiehall Street, Glasgow city centre.*

WC 🦮 ✕ FREE

🕐 All year, Mon–Sat, 9am–5pm. Sun, 11am–4.15pm.
Last orders 30 mins before closing.

Tel 0141 332 0521
www.willowtearooms.co.uk

University of Glasgow

THE WEST END

By the middle of the nineteenth century Glasgow faced a serious dilemma. The very industries that had helped create the wealth of the city, were making life there increasingly unpleasant. This was epitomised by the St Rollox chemical works, once the largest in Europe, which were built by Charles Tennant right in the city centre, just 457 metres from the Cathedral. People craved space and above all clean air. There was an attempt to copy Edinburgh and build a 'New Town' on the other side of the Clyde, connected to the centre by an elegant new suspension bridge that was built in 1851. But the grand project on the south bank never really took off and those that could afford it had begun migrating westwards.

The city fathers seemed to recognise this early on when they bought an 85-acre estate a mile or two west of the centre beside the River Kelvin for just under £100,000 in 1852. Kelvingrove Park was the first purpose-built park in Scotland and rapidly became a popular attraction. It was obviously open to all, but its setting in the West End helped divide Glasgow somewhat. The park's grand Victorian design by Sir Joseph Paxton is in sharp contrast to the flat grassland of Glasgow Green – the only real open space in the city's East End.

Beside the new park, a number of fine classical terraces began to spring up, notably around Woodland's Hill. Known as the Park Conservation Area just east of Kelvingrove, these streets have been described as one of the finest pieces of architectural planning of the nineteenth century. Grandest of all are Park Terrace and Park Quadrant, still among the smartest addresses in town with some of the best views thanks to their elevated position. The two great institutions that had been at the heart of Glasgow since the mid fifteenth century – the Old College and the Cathedral – stayed on in the centre. But in the 1870s, what was now Glasgow University gave up on its polluted surroundings and joined the stampede west. It moved into an awe-inspiring Gothic palazzo designed by Sir George Gilbert Scott between 1866-86. The structure was loosely based on the layout of the Old College and part of the old building was incorporated into the design such as the original gatehouse and the Lion and Unicorn balustrade. But the building's keynote, which has been the West End's greatest landmark ever since, was the Flemish Tower. Today you no longer have to enrol in order to look round the University – there is a visitor centre and various historical tours but many visitors come here to see the Hunterian Art Gallery. There is also a Zoology Museum in the Graham Kerr Building nearby. With the Kelvingrove Museum and Art Gallery and the Museum of Transport just a few blocks away, this corner of the West End holds some of the city's greatest visitor attractions.

Glasgow continued to spread westwards along the Great Western Road which runs straight as an arrow from St George's Cross, past the Botanic Gardens towards the suburbs where it turns into the A82, the road to Loch Lomond and the north. But the core of the West End has retained its village-like feel, especially since it was split off from the centre by the M8 motorway which snakes through the middle of Glasgow. With all its University students the area has a vaguely Bohemian air and is full of quirky boutiques, bars and independent restaurants, in contrast to the big chains who have taken over the centre. It's also very different from the overly residential South Side. Its main axis – the Byres Road that runs north from Kelvinhall to the Great Western Road – is a great place for a night-out and for week-end shopping. It is also well worth exploring the side streets, particularly those around Hillhead Underground station where some of the best bars and restaurants are to be found.

On the edge of the West End near the Forth & Clyde Canal, is one of Charles Rennie Mackintosh's less visited buildings. The Queen's Cross Church, which opened its doors in 1899, is well worth the trek however. The interplay between light and coloured glass clearly fascinated Mackintosh – something he put to good use in this church. On a fine day the interior looks magnificent with sunlight streaming through the stained-glass windows. The decoration is relatively simple and kept to some symbolic carving of stone and wood, but the overall effect is charming and in complete contrast to the clutter of earlier Victorian churches. Queen's Cross has its own information centre, being the headquarters of the Charles Rennie Mackintosh Society, together with a small shop and display area. The church also hosts the occasional concert.

Great Western Road Tenements

Hillhead Doorway

Loch Ard, Trossachs – with Ben Lomond in the distance

AROUND GLASGOW

Surrounded by all the stone, concrete and plate glass of this great, vibrant city, the countryside feels a long way off, and yet it is no great distance by car or train. And what comes as a delightful surprise to many as they leave Glasgow behind is just how wild and woolly the scenery becomes, especially if heading north. The Highland Boundary fault slants right across Scotland from the northeast almost clipping the edge of Glasgow en route.

You can even walk right into the Highlands from the city, or at least from its northern suburb of Milngavie. This is the start of the West Highland Way – the long-distance footpath that runs all the way to Fort William, 92 miles north. For anyone living in Britain's other big cities, the idea of being able to walk straight out into wild, open country is hard to imagine.

The biggest draw heading northwards is Loch Lomond, Britain's largest inland waterway. During the summer it seems half of Glasgow comes here at week-ends, but the crowds tend to stick to the west bank and the A82. The east bank is far less busy and makes a great place to come hill-walking – the whole area being part of the Loch Lomond and the Trossachs National Park. On a fine day the view over the Loch from the top of Ben Lomond (974m) is truly breathtaking. For gentler walks and some pretty villages to explore, the Campsie Fells to the east are even closer to Glasgow.

The main escape route and the city's umbilical cord to the rest of the world is of course the Clyde. At first Glasgow was held back by its river, which was too shallow to allow ships of any size to get close. Once the Clyde had been properly dredged, however, the city took off, first as a great trading port and then as an industrial powerhouse. But the river was never just about work. For whole generations of Glaswegians it meant the start of the holidays. Year after year families would go 'doon the watter' to the resorts on the Firth of Clyde. The annual migration to the likes of Dunoon, Gourock, Helensburgh and the Isle of Bute has dwindled to a trickle thanks to the advent of cheap air travel, but the resorts live on in all their glory. They are still being visited by the Waverley, the oldest sea-going paddle steamer in the world.

Heading upstream towards the source of the Clyde which rises 80 miles southeast of Glasgow, the landscape begins by showing the marks of heavy industries of the past. But that should not put anyone off visiting the World Heritage Site of New Lanark and the Falls of Clyde nearby. Just half an hour by train from Central Station, they make for a great day out.

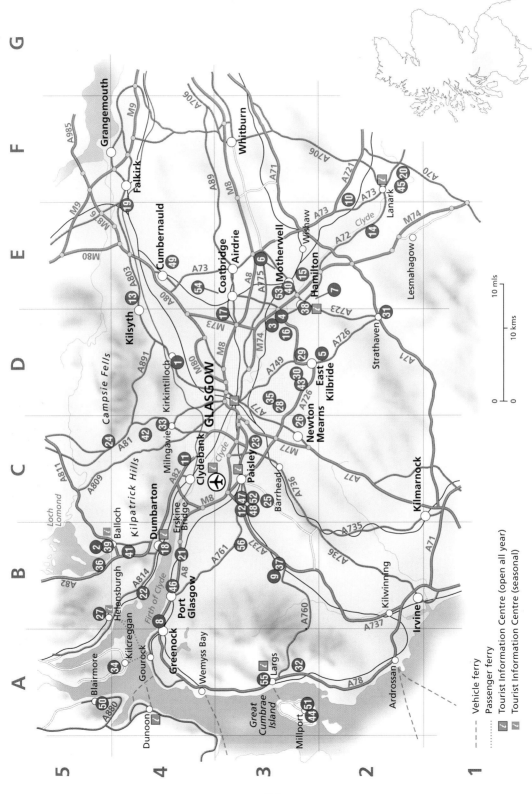

5 4 3 2 1

A B C D E F G

Grangemouth
A985
M9
Falkirk
M9
M876
M80
Whitburn
A706
A706
A71
A721
A70
Cumbernauld
19
A803
Kilsyth
13
A80
A73
A89
M8
A71
Wishaw
Lanark
45 20
M74
10
A73
Clyde
Lesmahagow
14
A72
M74
Coatbridge
Airdrie
49
A73
54
Motherwell
6
A8
A775
53 40
Hamilton
15
7
A723
38
Glasgow
1
M73
M8
M74
17
3 4
16
29
5
A749
43 30
A726
East
Kilbride
Strathaven
31
A71
Newton
Mearns
26
28
35
Paisley
23
Barrhead
25
Kilmarnock
M77
A77
A736
A735
A71
Milngavie
33
42
Kirkintilloch
A891
24
A81
Campsie Fells
A809
Kilpatrick Hills
Clydebank
11
A82
M8
Dumbarton
18
21
56
A761
A737
9 37
Kilwinning
A760
Irvine
A737
Loch
Lomond
2
39
41
36
Balloch
A811
A814
22
46
A8
Port
Glasgow
8
Greenock
Helensburgh
27
Gourock
Kilcreggan
34
Blairmore
50
A880
Dunoon
Wemyss Bay
Largs
55
32
A78
Ardrossan
Great
Cumbrae
Island
44 51
Millport
12 41
48 52

Firth of Clyde
Erskine
Bridge

Clyde

A985

Scale:
0 — 10 mls
0 — 10 kms

- - - - Vehicle ferry
.... Passenger ferry
Tourist Information Centre (open all year)
Tourist Information Centre (seasonal)

64

ATTRACTIONS AROUND GLASGOW

1 Auld Kirk Museum

The Auld Kirk, built in 1644, now houses the principal museum for East Dunbartonshire. The recently refurbished museum highlights Kirkintilloch's history from the Roman times to the present including displays on the industrial age of the Lion Foundry and Canal Boatyards, home of the famous Clyde Puffers.

D4 *Kirkintilloch Cross, Kirkintilloch off the A803.*

🅿 🚾 ♿ ⛪ E AV FREE

🕑 All year, Tue–Sat, 10am–1pm & 2–5pm.

Tel 0141 578 0144
www.eastdunbarton.gov.uk

2 Balloch Castle Country Park

Balloch Castle Country Park, once the stronghold of one of Scotland's most powerful medieval families, is now a gateway to Loch Lomond National Park. With two hundred acres of varied countryside, a visitor centre and ranger service you can explore woodlands, parkland and gardens. Work is ongoing in some of the garden areas to restore the park to its former glory.

B5 *S end of Loch Lomond on A811, off A82*

🅿 🚾 ⛪ 🏕 🚶 🧗 🎣 FREE

🕑 Country Park, all year round, daily.
Visitor Centre: Easter–Oct, daily, 10am.
Closing times vary, please check.

Tel 01389 722600
www.lochlomond-trossachs.org

3 Bothwell Castle

This, the largest thirteenth-century stone castle in Scotland, consisted of a courtyard surrounded by a series of towers. Bothwell Castle suffered great damage during the Wars of Independence due to sieges, surrenders and demolitions, but part of the original circular keep still survives.

D3 *At Uddingston off the B7071.*

🅿 🚾 ⛪ E 🏕 🧗 🎣 £

🕑 Apr–Sept, daily, 9.30am–6.30pm.
Oct–Mar, Sat–Wed, 9.30am–4.30pm.

Tel 01698 816894   www.historic-scotland.gov.uk

Bothwell Castle & the River Clyde

4 Bothwell Parish Church ✠

Ancient and historic church of architectural and ecclesiastical importance, known as the Cathedral of Lanarkshire. Founded in the 6th century by Archibald, 3rd Earl of Douglas, the present building dates from 1398 and contains notable stained-glass windows and embroideries, known as the 'Bothwell Embroideries'.

D3 *Off A725, Main Street, Bothwell, nine miles S of Glasgow.*

P WC & ● FREE

⏱ Sun, for worship; May–Aug, daily 10.30am–12.30 & 2–4pm.

Tel 01698 853189

5 Calderglen Country Park ♣

A suitable destination for a family outing, with a children's zoo containing an assortment of animals, play areas and an adventure playground. There are miles of country trails including walks along the River Calder, several waterfalls and interesting geological features. A visitor centre houses an audio-visual room, history room, gallery and a wildlife display. A variety of events are held throughout the year.

D2 *S of East Kilbride on A726.*

P WC & ● ♨ E AV ♩ ☀ ♟ ☎ FREE

⏱ Park: dawn–dusk. Visitor centre: Summer, Mon–Fri 10.30am–5pm; Sat, Sun & Public Holidays 10.30am–5.30pm. Conservatory, Apr–Sept, daily 10am–8pm; Oct–Mar, daily 10am–4.30pm.

Tel 01355 236644

6 Carfin Grotto and Pilgrimage Centre 🏛

Carfin Grotto is a shrine to St Therese of Lisieux and was created by unemployed Catholic miners in 1922 as a copy of the shrine of Our Lady of Lourdes. The adjacent visitor centre looks at the history and traditions of pilgrimage in Scotland and around the world. Visual displays offer the opportunity to explore world faiths including Christianity, Judaism, Buddhism, Hinduism, Sikhism and Islam.

E3 *Carfin, 12m E of Glasgow, off the A73.*

P WC & ✕ ♨ E AV ☎ FREE

⏱ Mar–Dec, daily, 10am–5pm. Jan & Feb, Mon–Fri, 10am–5pm.

Tel 01698 268941   www.rcdom.org.uk

7 Chatelherault Country Park ♣

Chatelherault is an eighteenth-century hunting lodge and summer-house, originally commissioned by the fifth Duke of Hamilton. Restored in the 1980s, along with formal gardens and a museum, visitors can also see the Duke's banqueting hall and bedroom. Woodland walks provide access to the gorge of the River Avon, ancient oaks and ruined Cadzow Castle. Walks and activities led by a ranger service are offered.

E3 *Enter at village of Ferniegair, on A72.*

P WC & ● ♨ E ♩ ☀ ♟ FREE

⏱ Visitor Centre: Mon–Sat, 10am–5pm; Sun 12 noon–5pm. House: Mon–Thur, 10am–4.30pm; Sun 12 noon–4.30pm. Closed Fri & Sat. Park: all year round, daylight hours.

Tel 01698 426213

8 Clyde Marine Cruises ★

Cruise spectacular West Coast scenery aboard the *Second Snark*, with day trips to the islands of Arran, Bute, Cumbrae and the Highland village of Tignabruaich. The *Second Snark* was built in 1938 and is one of the few remaining working examples of its type, and is listed on the Historic Ships Register.

B4 *All sailings depart from Victoria Harbour, Greenock. Three trains per hour run to Greenock from Glasgow Central.*

P WC ● £££

⏱ Day trips operate from Jun–Aug, see website or phone for details of routes and timetables.

Tel 01475 721281   www.clyde-marine.co.uk

9 Clyde Muirshiel Regional Park ♣

Clyde Muirshiel Regional Park covers 106 square miles of countryside that includes woodlands, moorlands, lochs and coastlines. Individual centres within the Park are staffed by experienced countryside rangers and outdoor instructors. Outdoor activities on offer include water sports, mountain bike hire, fishing, woodland walks and nature trails. Visitors can also visit historical sites such as chambered burial cairns, a roman road and copper and barytes mines.

B3   *Off the A737 E of Largs at Lochwinnoch.*

🅿 ♿ ♿ 🍴 🎁 ⛺ ❄ 🏃 🎫 FREE

🕐 Visitor Centre: Apr–Oct, daily, 10am–8pm or dusk.
Nov–Mar, 10am–4pm. Check website for activities
and charges

Tel 01505 842882
www.clydemuirshiel.co.uk

10   Clyde Valley Woodlands

A National Nature Reserve featuring a mix
of ash, oak and elm trees. The reserve's steep
gorges have protected the woodlands from
felling and provides a fertile home for wildlife,
especially birds and plants. Care should be
taken on its often steep path network.

F2   *Off A72, on outskirts of Carluke or A706/A72,
outskirts of Lanark.*

❄ 🎫 FREE

🕐 Open access.

Tel 01555 665928
www.snh.org.uk or clydevalleywoods.org.uk

11   Clydebank Museum

Clydebank Museum is home to three major
exhibitions: shipbuilding, the Clydebank Blitz
and Singer sewing machines. Shipbuilding tells
the story of Clydebank's many world-famous
ships, and visitors can experience what life was
like in the shipyards. The Clydebank Blitz brings
to life the effects the bombing of March 1941
had on the people of the area. The museum
also houses the sewing machine collection and
technical archive of the Singer Manufacturing
Company, donated in 1980 when the company
left Clydebank.

C4   *Town Hall, Clydebank on the A814.*

♿ ♿ 🎁 E FREE

🕐 Open all year, Mon, Wed, Thur & Fri, 2pm–4.30pm.
Tue & Sat 10am–4.30pm.
Closed public holidays.

Tel 01389 738702

12   Coats Observatory

Built by John Honeyman, this Victorian
observatory focusses on astronomy, astronautics,
meteorology, seismology and the history and
architecture of the building. In addition to

meteorological and astronomical information,
which have been recorded at the Observatory
since 1882, continuous seismic activity recording
is carried out. Public astronomical viewing is on
Thursday evenings in winter, weather permitting.

C3   *Oakshaw Street, Paisley.*

♿ E FREE

🕐 All year round, Tue–Sat, 10am–5pm;
Sun 2–5pm. Oct–Mar, Thur, weather permitting,
7pm–9.30pm.

Tel 0141 889 2013
www.renfrewshire.gov.uk

13   Colzium Estate

Colzium Estate dates from the twelfth century
and has an extensive collection of trees and
shrubs in an Arboretum and a display of conifers
and rare plants in the Walled Garden. The ruins
of Colzium Castle, a fifteenth-century L-plan
tower house, along with a renovated ice-house,
curling pond and the 'Clock Theatre' are also
featured on the estate.

E4   *Off the A803 Stirling Road, Kilsyth NE of Glasgow
city centre.*

🅿 ♿ ♿ ❄ FREE

🕐 Estate open all year, dawn to dusk.
House & Museum by arrangement,
limited disabled access.
Walled garden, Apr–Sep, Mon–Fri, 12noon–7pm.
Sat & Sun, 1–4pm.

Tel 01698 266155
www.northlan.gov.uk

14   Craignethan Castle

Set by the River Nethan, Craignethan was
originally built by Sir James Hamilton of Finnart
around 1530. As part of its importance as an
early artillery fortification, the castle's defences
include a 'caponier', a stone vaulted artillery
chamber, unique in Britain. Various additions
were made over the next few hundred years,
including a tower house, which is still in
reasonable condition.

E2   *5.5 miles WNW of Lanark off the A72.*

🅿 ♿ 🍴 🎁 E ⛺ £

🕐 Apr–Sept, daily, 9.30am–6.30pm.
Oct–Mar, open weekends only, 9.30am–4.30pm.
Last admission 30 mins before closing.

Tel 01555 860364
www.historic-scotland.gov.uk

15 Dalzell Estate

Originally a Royal Hunting Forest owned by the Dalzell family, the estate now features woodland walks and a Japanese Garden created in the 1920s. Also located here is the Covenanter's Oak, under whose branches religious services were held during the seventeenth century, and an Arboreteum which has a collection of exotic and indigenous trees.

E3 *Adele Road, Motherwell, off the B754 E of Glasgow city centre.*

P ♨ ⚇ FREE

⊕ Estate open all year, dawn to dusk.
   Limited car parking facilities.

01698 266155   www.northlan.gov.uk

16 David Livingstone Centre

Scotland's famous explorer was born in this one-room tenement in 1813 and today it houses a museum devoted to him. David Livingstone's childhood home remains much as it would have been in his day and gives the visitor an insight into the living conditions endured by industrial workers in the nineteenth century. Visitors can learn about Livingstone's explorations and see a number of personal items including diaries, navigational equipment and even the red shirt he was wearing when he met the journalist H M Stanley.

D3 *Blantyre, off M74 at J5, via A725/A724.*

P WC ⚇ ☕ ⌂ E ⚇ £

⊕ 1 Apr–24 Dec, Mon–Sat, 10am–5pm; Sun 12.30–5pm.

Tel 01698 823140   www.nts.org.uk

17 Drumpellier Country Park

Covering an area of 500 acres, Drumpellier Country Park contains two lochs, lowland heath, mixed woodlands and open grassland. The area is rich in wildlife and is also a Site of Special Scientific Interest. There are nature trails, gardens, picnic sites and childrens play areas. The visitor centre has a cafeteria and displays on the natural history of the area.

D3 *Townhead Road, Coatbridge off the A752, E of Glasgow city centre.*

P WC ⚇ ☕ ⌂ ♨ ⚇ FREE

⊕ Visitor Centre: Apr, May & Sept, 10.30am–5pm.
   Jun, Jul & Aug, 10.30am–7.30pm.
   Oct–Mar, 10.30am–4pm.
   Closed 25, 26 Dec & 1, 2 Jan.
   Park: all year, 9am–dusk.
   Charges apply to some activities.

Tel 01698 266155   www.northlan.gov.uk

18 Dumbarton Castle

Dumbarton was the centre of the ancient kingdom of Strathclyde from the fifth century until 1018. Once an important royal refuge, the castle remains lie on Dumbarton Rock, a volcanic plug measuring around 73m (250ft), above the Firth of Clyde.

B4 *Dumbarton on the A82.*

P WC ☕ ⌂ E ♨ £

⊕ Apr–Sept, daily, 9.30am–6.30pm.
   Oct–Mar, 9.30am–4.30pm, closed Thur & Fri.

Tel 01389 732167
www.historic-scotland.gov.uk

Dumbarton Rock and Castle

DOON THE WATTER

The mid nineteenth century saw Glasgow expand at a rapid rate, with an influx of population from both the Highlands and Ireland. Poor housing and cramped working conditions meant that people craved an escape from the city in the summer months. This led to the tradition of going 'doon the watter' or down the Clyde by steamship. Rail and ferry links were being developed at this same time, allowing for the emergence of a tourist industry on the islands

Mount Stuart, Isle of Bute

and coastal resorts along and below the Clyde. By the end of the century many factories and shipyards closed for a week to give their workforce an unpaid break. Workers would save their money with Friendly Societies to pay for the annual holiday.

Families would board a steamship in Glasgow for a day out – or for longer. Many of the ships were in fact chartered by temperance societies, keen to promote an alcohol-free trip at a time when drinking was an inner-city problem. The *Waverley* is the oldest ocean-going paddle steamer in the world today and still makes regular trips down the Clyde during the summer months. The legacy of these early days

of steamships can be seen on board the vessel.

The main destinations were Gourock, Dunoon, Wemyss Bay, the Isle of Bute, Helensburgh and Ardrossan. Many still have the same tourist infrastructure developed by the Victorians – namely the piers and promenades, the small hotels and bed & breakfast places and the funfairs, parks and gardens. In their wake came dozens of fish and chip shops and ice-cream parlours often run by Italian immigrant families like the Nardinis, whose art-deco café is one of the attractions in Largs.

One of the favourite destinations was Rothesay on the Isle of Bute when up to a hundred steamers a day would arrive in the resort's heyday. The first port of call for male visitors was often the Gents on the pier – a magnificent public convenience, with green marble, gleaming copper and beautiful mosaics. Today, female visitors can come and view them at appointed times.

The popularity of going 'Doon the Watter' began to fade with people's greater prosperity and the advent of cheap charter flights to the continent in the 1960s. With unpredictable weather and little chance of a sun tan, the Costa del Clyde lost its appeal. Ferries continue to operate out of Gourock and Wemys Bay, but only the *Waverley* still sails from Glasgow.

Dunoon Pier

THE FALKIRK WHEEL

Some 45 minutes by car to the east of Glasgow, just outside Falkirk, lies one of Scotland's most extraordinary feats of modern engineering: **The Falkirk Wheel**. It was opened by the Queen in 2002 and is the link between two of Scotland's major canals – the Forth & Clyde and the Union Canal. They both played important roles in the industrial development of central Scotland from the late eighteenth century. Now the physical link between both canals has been developed as a year-round visitor attraction.

First came the Forth & Clyde Canal, built during the 1780s and designed as a 35-mile link between the river Clyde and the Forth estuary near Grangemouth. The Union Canal opened 40 years later, starting in Edinburgh and running the 30 miles to Falkirk where a system of locks connected both canal routes. Coal, iron and other key raw materials were carried by barges, providing the backbone to Scotland's industrial development during the nineteenth century.

The age of the train and later the motorcar brought about the demise of the canal as a transport system and the Falkirk link fell into disrepair. In the late 1990s, however, with increased interest in leisure and conservation, it was decided to restore the lock system at Falkirk into an ambitious engineering project – the Millennium Link – now known as the Falkirk Wheel.

Costing nearly £90 million, the 'wheel' is in fact a massive gondola which transports whole barges or pleasure craft from one canal to the other. The structure is 115 feet high (35 metres). Boats are manoeuvred into a kind of cradle which contains around 300 tonnes of water, which then slowly rotates. One admirer described it as 'the largest piece of functional sculpture' in the world. Alongside the lower basin is an excellent visitor centre, gift shop and café from where you can watch the uplifting of the boats or go on a brief sail on a barge to experience it for yourself. A play area for children and walks and trails along the canals add to the attractions of this site.

19 Falkirk Wheel ★

This huge engineering wonder connects the Forth & Clyde and Union Canals which run between Edinburgh and Glasgow. Its rotating gondola structure literally lifts boats from one canal to another. Members of the public can witness the wheel in motion from the well equipped visitor centre, or experience it for real on organised boat trips. See feature on page 70.

E4 *On the outskirts of Falkirk, off A803 or M9 at J6.*

P WC & ♥ ✕ ⌂ E AV ⛱ ☃ 🚶 ♿ £££

⏰ Visitor Centre: Apr–Nov, daily, 9am–6pm. Nov–Mar 9am–5pm. Last admission 30 min before closing. Boat trips from 9.30am–5pm, booking recommended.

Booking Line: 08700 500208
www.falkirkwheel.co.uk

20 Falls of Clyde Wildlife Reserve 🐦 🦦

The reserve's woodlands are managed by the Scottish Wildlife Trust and cover an area of 150 acres. The River Clyde flows through the gorge creating several impressive waterfalls, the largest of which is the Corra Linn with a drop of 26 m (84 ft). The reserve is home to a number of wildlife species including a wide range of birds, deer, foxes and badgers. The visitor centre offers a ranger service which provides a number of outdoor activities and events such as badger watching, peregrine falcon viewing and guided walks to learn about the diverse flora and fauna of the reserve.

F2 *From M74, follow signs for New Lanark.*

P ⌂ E ☃ 🚶 FREE

⏰ Visitor Centre: daily; Mar–Dec, 11am–5pm; Jan–Feb, 12noon–4pm. Reserve: daily; summer, 8am–8pm; winter, during daylight hours.

Tel 01555 665262   www.swt.org.uk

21 Finlaystone Country Estate 🌳

Built in the fourteenth century and extended in 1760 and again in 1900, Finlaystone House is currently home to the Chief of the Clan MacMillan. Extensive grounds contain formal gardens, woodland walks and play areas. The visitor centre houses a collection of dolls from around the world and the history of Clan MacMillan.

B4 *On A8, one mile W of Langbank.*

P WC & ♥ ⌂ E ⛱ ☃ 🚶 £

⏰ Grounds: all year round, daily, 10.30am–5pm. House: to groups by appointment only. Visitor Centre, daily, Apr–Sep, 11am–5pm. Oct–Dec, 11am–4pm. Jan–Mar, Sat–Sun, 12noon–4pm.

Tel 01475 540505
www.finlaystone.co.uk

22 Geilston Garden 🌷 ❀

Geilston was laid out over 200 years ago and is set around a seventeenth-century house (not open to the public). The walled garden contains shrub borders, lawns and a herbaceous border that provides an abundance of colours in summer. Fruit, vegetables and flowers are grown in the kitchen garden and the Geilston Burn runs through the gardens where visitors can also enjoy woodland walks.

B4 *On A814, at west end of Cardross, 18 miles NW of Glasgow*

P WC & ☃ 🚶 £

⏰ Apr–Oct, daily, 9.30am–5pm. Limited disabled access to some areas of the garden.

Tel 01389 849187   www.nts.org.uk

23 Glasgow Museums Resource Centre

Glasgow Museums Resource Centre is the first publicly accessible store for the City's museum service and gives visitors a behind-the-scenes look at 200,000 treasures held in storage, ranging from art to botanical specimens. Access to the stores is by guided tour only, which are held daily at 2.30pm. Viewing of specific objects or artwork can be arranged by special request (at least two weeks' notice is required). Please contact the Resource Centre for further information about upcoming activities, special tours and talks.

C3 *Woodhead Road, Nitshill, from Glasgow city centre, take the M77, off at J3 and follow signs for Paisley.*

P WC & FREE

⏰ Mon–Thur & Sat, 10am–5pm. Fri & Sun, 11am–5pm. Guided tours daily at 2.30pm.

Tel 0141 276 9300
www.glasgowmuseums.com

24 Glengoyne Distillery

Visitors can tour this 150-year-old distillery, built on the edge of the Campsie Fells, and learn the secrets behind malting, mashing, fermentation and distillation, before sampling the end product, Glengoyne single malt whisky.

C5 *On A81, three miles N of Strathblane.*

P WC & 🏛 E AV 🎋 🏃 🎟

⏲ All year, daily; Tours, 10am–4pm, every hour. Sun 12pm–4pm.
Shop: Mon–Sat, 09.30am–5pm. Sun 12.30–5pm.
Telephone for Xmas/New Year opening times.

Tel 01360 550254
www.glengoyne.com

25 Gleniffer Braes Country Park

An upland park associated with the 18th-and 19th-century weaver poets. Covering an area of approximately 1300 acres, it is mainly moorland but has forested areas. It is home to a variety of wildlife, and visitors can explore the gorge, various marked trails and play areas, and admire panoramic views.

C3 *Glenfield Road, Paisley off the B775.*

P WC E 🎋 🏃 FREE

⏲ Daily, 8am–dusk.

Tel 0141 884 3794
www.renfrewshire.gov.uk

26 Greenbank Garden

Greenbank consists of over 15 acres of gardens which surround a Georgian house, built in 1764 and originally the home of a Glasgow merchant. On display are a range of ornamental plants, annuals, perennials, shrubs and trees demonstrating the wide variety of plants which can be grown in the area.

C3 *Off M77 and A726, follow signs for East Kilbride to Clarkston Toll; six miles S of Glasgow city centre.*

WC & ☕ 🏛 🎋 🏃 ££

⏲ Gardens open all year, daily, 9.30am–sunset.
Tearoom/shop: Apr–Oct, daily, 11am–5pm.
Nov–Mar, weekends, 2–4pm.
House: Apr–Oct, Sun, 2–4.pm

Tel 0141 616 5126   www.nts.org.uk

27 The Hill House

The Hill House is considered Charles Rennie Mackintosh's finest domestic creation. Most of the original furniture and fittings are still in place, including designs by Margaret Macdonald Mackintosh. In addition to Mackintosh's striking interiors, there are changing exhibitions featuring the work of young designers.
The gardens, which command views over the Clyde, have been restored and reflect features common to Mackintosh's architectural designs. See feature pages 42–47.

B5 *On the eastern edge of Helensburgh. Off B832, between A82 and A814. 23m NW of Glasgow.*

P & ☕ 🏛 E 🎋 🏃 🎟 £££

⏲ Apr–Oct, daily, 1.30pm–5.30pm.

Tel 01436 673900
www.nts.org.uk

28 Holmwood House

This, perhaps the finest example of Alexander 'Greek' Thomson's domestic designs, was built in a classical Greek style in 1857 for James Couper, a local paper-mill owner. The continuing conservation work to the building has uncovered many of Thomson's original decorative designs, including much of the wall stencilling. A small Victorian kitchen garden and wildflower-rich woodland are also a feature of the property. See feature, page 57.

D3 *Netherlee Road, four miles S of Glasgow city centre; signposted from Clarkston Road on B767.*

P WC & ☕ 🏛 E 🏃 ££

⏲ Mar–Oct, 1.30–5.30pm.
Groups must pre–book.

Tel 0141 637 2129
www.nts.org.uk

The Hill House, Helensburgh

29 Hunter House Museum

This interactive museum tells the story of John and William Hunter, born here in the eighteenth century. Both made their fame and fortune in the world of medicine and science. The New Town display area describes how East Kilbride became Scotland's first 'new town', and features old photographs and audio.

D3 *Maxwellton Road, NE of East Kilbride town centre; off A749 to Calderwood Road.*

P ☕ E FREE

🕐 Apr–Sept, Mon–Fri, 12.30–4.30pm; weekends 12 noon–5pm.

Tel 01355 261261

30 James Hamilton Heritage Park

This country park features a 16 acre loch and a bird sanctuary, a visitor centre and children's play area. Watersport facilities include sailing dinghies, pedaloes, kayaks and canoes, rowing boats and bumper boats. Sailboats and windsurfing boards are available for hire.

D3 *Stewartfield Way, East Kilbride.*

P wc ⛱ ♨ ⚐ FREE

🕐 Watersports centre; April–Oct.
Visitor Centre; Easter–Oct. Telephone for details.

Tel 01355 276611

31 John Hastie Museum

Sitting on the edge of Strathaven Park, this local museum dates back to the 1920s. It features displays on life in the area including its agricultural and weaving history, and also Strathaven's link to the Covenanters and the Battle of Drumclog. Information on walks, trails and cycle tracks in the area.

D2 *Threestanes Road, Strathaven, on the A71 NE of Kilmarnock.*

E FREE

🕐 Apr–Sept, daily, 12.30–4.30pm.

Tel 01357 521257

32 Kelburn Castle & Country Centre

Kelburn Castle, family home of the Earls of Glasgow, dates back to the thirteenth century and is surrounded by parkland. Tours of the castle are available. Activities include walks and trails, horse riding, pets' corner, falconry centre, play areas and the 'Secret Forest' adventure area. A ranger service organises guided walks and many other activities.

A3 *Off A78, two miles S of Largs.*

P & ✕ 🏛 AV ⛱ ♨ ⚐ ££

🕐 Country Centre, daily, Apr–Oct 10am–6pm.
Secret Forest, daily from12noon.
Castle, end Jun–Mid Sept.
Nov–Mar, grounds & riding school only, 11am–dusk.
Closed Christmas Day, Boxing Day and New Year's Day.

Tel 01475 568685

www.kelburncountrycentre.com

33 Lillie Art Gallery

A purpose-built gallery which opened in 1962 funded by a bequest from local banker and artist, Robert Lillie (1867-1949). It houses a collection of Scottish art from the 1880s to the present day. The gallery mounts temporary exhibitions including thematic exhibitions from the galleries permanent collection and touring exhibitions by contemporary Scottish artists. There are children's Saturday morning art classes and other educational activities.

C4 *Station Road, Milngavie off the A81 NW of Glasgow .*

P wc & 🏛 E FREE

🕐 All year, Tues–Sat 10am–1pm & 2pm–5pm.

Tel 0141 578 8847

34 Linn Botanic Gardens

The gardens, situated on the mild west coast, contain around 8000 varieties of ferns, conifers and flowering plants collected from around the world. Features include a bamboo garden, formal and informal ponds, a rhododendron gully, herbaceous borders, rockery and cliff gardens. There are views of the Firth of Clyde and a nursery sells plants.

A4 *3/4 mile N of Cove village, by Helensburgh, on the B313.*

P 🏛 ⛱ ♨ ⚐ £

🕐 Open all year, dawn to dusk.

Tel 01436 842242

35 Linn Park

Linn Park is the second-largest park in Glasgow. Its area of 203 acres ranges from open grassland to woodlands and riversides. Facilities include a countryside ranger centre with events and activities throughout the year, an equestrian centre, woodland and river walks, orienteering course, 18-hole golf course and children's play areas.

D3 *Simshill Road off the B762 S of Glasgow city centre.*

🅿 📶 🚶 FREE

🕐 All year, dawn to dusk.

Tel 0141 637 1147
www.glasgow.gov.uk

36 Loch Lomond Shores ★

This visitor attraction forms a gateway for 'Loch Lomond and the Trossachs National Park'. Its 'Drumkinnon Tower' features exhibitions, film shows and viewing galleries over Loch Lomond, as well as shopping and dining. The adjacent 'National Park Gateway Centre' is staffed by Park Rangers and contains a tourist information centre. It offers displays and further advice on how to enjoy the diverse range of activities available both locally and throughout the whole of the national park. See Loch Lomond feature on page 76.

B5 *Leave M8 at J30 Erskine Bridge. Join the A82 and follow signs for Balloch (approx14m).*

🅿 📶 ♿ ☕ ✕ 🏛 E 📹 🍴 🌿 🚶 🚼 ££

🕐 Open all year, daily, Apr–Oct, 10am–6pm.
Closed 25 December.
Charge for entry to Beneath the Loch, Legend of the Loch and the Drumkinnon Tower.

Tel 01389 722406
www.lochlomondshores.com

37 Lochwinnoch RSPB Nature Reserve 🐦

Situated within the Clyde Muirshiel Regional Park, Lochwinnoch is one of the few remaining wetland sites in West Scotland. Nature trails and hides allow visitors to view the varied species of birds and wildlife that frequent the reserve. The visitor centre has a ground-level viewing area with binoculars and telescopes. The viewing tower offers panoramic views over the Aird meadow and features informative and interactive displays. A variety of events run throughout the year.

B3 *SW of Glasgow off the A737 Irvine Road between Paisley and Largs.*

🅿 📶 ♿ 🏛 🍴 🌿 🚼 📼 £

🕐 Reserve: open access.
Visitor centre: daily, 10am–5pm.
Closed 25, 26 December & 1, 2 Jan.

Tel 01505 842663
www.rspb.org.uk

38 Low Parks Museum

Two museums in one, housed in historic buildings which were once part of the Duke of Hamilton's estate. The area's history is explored through a changing programme of exhibitions, events, displays and interactives, while an exhibition gives an insight into the history of the Cameronians (Scottish Rifles) Regiment through a series of displays and reconstructions.

E3 *Muir Street, Hamilton, off J6 of the M74.*

🅿 📶 ♿ 🏛 E FREE

🕐 Open all year, Mon–Sat, 10am–5pm;
Sun 12 noon–5pm.
Telephone for Christmas/New Year closing.
Tours of the Hamilton Mausoleum, Sat, Sun & Wed 3pm in summer and 2pm in winter.

Tel 01698 328232
www.southlanarkshire.gov.uk

39 Maid of the Loch ★

Launched in 1953, the *Maid of the Loch* is the last paddle steamer and the largest inland waterway passenger vessel to be built in Britain. A trust was set up in 1996 to restore the *Maid* and to put her back into service on Loch Lomond. Visitors can now visit the vessel and see the continuing restoration work.

B5 *Pier Road, Balloch*

🅿 📶 ♿ ☕ 🏛 E FREE

🕐 Apr–Oct, daily, 11am–4pm.
Nov–Mar, Sat & Sun, 11am–4pm.
Restricted wheelchair access.

Tel 01389 711865
www.maidoftheloch.co.uk

LOCH LOMOND AND THE TROSSACHS NATIONAL PARK

In 1795 John Aspinwall, great grandfather of US President Franklin Rooseveldt, climbed to the top of Ben Lomond and declared the loch below was 'the finest body of sweet water in Scotland ... forming an uncommonly romantic scene.' A few decades later Sir Walter Scott reinforced this view in his epic poem 'The Lady of the Lake' and his romantic novel *Rob Roy*. Both works promoted Loch Lomond and the Trossachs to a vast readership. With added help from the famous Jacobite ballad about the Loch's 'bonnie banks', and the start of package tours to the area in 1850 by Thomas Cook, people have been flocking here ever since.

The Loch is Britain's largest inland waterway, 22 miles long and up to 5 miles wide. At the southern end of the Loch, is the resort town of Balloch, just 20 miles north of Glasgow and departure point for countless boat trips. It is also home to Loch Lomond Shores – a massive new visitor centre and shopping complex by the water's edge.

At its core stands Drumkinnon Tower, whose sixth-floor gallery offers a spectacular view looking north up the Loch straight into the Highlands. Along with permanent film shows about the legends of the Loch above and below the surface, there are restaurants, exhibitions and a regular farmers' market. There is also a well-equipped tourist office and ranger service, this being the gateway to Scotland's first National Park.

Opened in 2002, Loch Lomond and the Trossachs National Park stretches from the Cowal Penisular in the west to Loch Earn in the east. The Campsie Fells, an area of gentle rolling hills that was once bandit country in the days of Rob Roy, lies between the northern suburbs of Glasgow and the Carse of Stirling farmland to the north. Local attractions include the pretty village of Fintry, the **Glengoyne** whisky distillery and various walks. Hill-walking is also popular on the east side of Loch Lomond, particularly Ben Lomond (974m), the most southerly Munro. The west bank of the Loch is very different with a succession of hotels, caravan parks and marinas lining the often congested A82.

40 Motherwell Heritage Centre

This award-winning heritage centre opened in 1996, and features a semicircular building with an 18m high viewing tower. 'Technoplus' is a hands-on permanent exhibition telling the story of the growth of the area from the arrival of the Romans, to the Industrial Revolution, and to the present day. The 'Local History' room contains archive material, with staff on hand to advise on family and local history research. There are temporary exhibitions throughout the year.

E3 *High Road, Motherwell, Motherwell Junction off the M74.*

🅿 🚾 ♿ 🏛 E ⅍ FREE

🕐 All year round, Wed, Fri & Sat, 10am–5pm.
   Thur 10am–7pm.
   Sun 12noon–5pm.
   Open Mon Public Holidays.

Tel 01698 251000
www.northlan.gov.uk

41 Motoring Heritage Centre

The Heritage Centre is housed in the marble building of The Argyll Motor Works, which in 1905 was the world's largest car factory, covering an area of 11 acres. Visitors can discover the story of Scotland's motoring heritage and its sporting heroes through archive film, interpretative displays and memorabilia. Many Scottish-built cars are on display along with a 1925 Model T Ford which visitors can sit in.

B4 *Loch Lomond Outlet Shopping Centre, Alexandria, 18m NW of Glasgow.*

🅿 🚾 ♿ ✗ 🏛 E £

🕐 All year, daily, Mon–Sat, 9.30am–5.30am.
   Sun, 11am – 5pm.
   Closed 25 Dec & 1 Jan.

Tel 01380 607862
www.motoringheritage.co.uk

42 Mugdock Country Park 🌳

A country park stretching through a variety of landscapes, and incorporating Mugdock Castle, Loch and the ruins of Craigend Castle. Visitors can make use of paths, gardens, play areas and a ranger service. While the visitor centre has information on the history and wildlife of the park, the ranger service organises events and activities throughout the year from pond dipping to history tours and jazz evenings.

C4 *Follow A81 Glasgow/Strathblane Road; signposted from Canniesburn.*

🅿 🚾 ♿ 💬 ✗ 🏛 E 🆎 🏮 ⅍ 🚶 🆔 FREE

🕐 Visitor Centre, daily, 9am–9pm.
   Winter, closes 6pm.

Tel 0141 956 6100
www.mugdock-country-park.org.uk

43 Museum of Scottish Country Life

The Museum of Scottish Country Life is comprised of a musem and working farm. You can explore the National Country Life Collection in the museum to learn how country people in Scotland lived and worked in the past. The Georgian farmhouse and working farm at Wester Kittochside, owned by the Reid family since the sixteenth century, was gifted to the National Trust for Scotland in 1992. It illustrates how farming still shapes the countryside of Scotland today. The farm is worked using techniques and equipment of the 1950s, complete with all the sights, smells and sounds of a working farm.

D3 *Wester Kittochside, East Kilbride. Off Junction 5 of the M74.*

🅿 🚾 ♿ 💬 🏛 E 🏮 ⅍ 🚶 🆔 ££

🕐 Daily, 10am–5pm.
   Closed 25, 26 Dec & 1, 2 Jan.

Tel 01355 224181
www.nms.ac.uk/country

44 Museum of the Cumbraes

Visitors can learn about life on the islands of Great and Little Cumbrae with a display of old photographs and artefacts, showing the islands' history and Millport's past as a holiday destination.

A3 *Millport, on B899, on the Isle of Cumbrae; a ferry runs from Largs.*

🅿 🚾 ♿ E FREE

🕐 Apr–Sep, Thur–Mon, 10am–1pm & 2–5pm.

Tel 01475 531 191
www.north-ayrshire.gov.uk

45 New Lanark World Heritage Village

Surrounded by native woodlands and close to the Falls of Clyde, this cotton mill village was founded in 1785 and became famous as the site of Robert Owen's model community. Now fully restored as both a living community and visitor attraction, the history of the village is interpreted in an award-winning visitor centre with a dark ride called The New Millennium Experience and the show Annie McLeod's Story, which tells the story of New Lanark in the 1820s. There are also a Village store, millmakers' and Robert Owen's houses. New Lanark is now protected as a World Heritage site. See feature page 79.

F2 By Lanark, off A73

P ᵂᶜ ♿ ⬤ ✕ ⬛ E ⌒ ⚹ ⚸ ⊞ £

🕐 All year round, daily, 11am–5pm. Closed 25 Dec & 1 Jan. 12 noon–4 pm, 26 Dec & 2 Jan.

Tel 01555 661345   www.newlanark.org

46 Newark Castle

Dating back to the fifteenth century, Newark was once occupied by James IV in the 1490s. The gatehouse tower was later joined to a mansion block by Patrick Maxwell, creating an elegant Renaissance house.

B4 Port Glasgow on the A8; turn right at Newark roundabout.

P ᵂᶜ ⬛ E £

🕐 Apr–Sept, daily, 9.30am–6.30pm.
Oct–Mar, Mon–Sat, 9.30am–4.30pm.

Tel 01475 741858   www.historic-scotland.gov.uk

47 Paisley Abbey ✠

Paisley Abbey was founded in 1163 as a Monastery of the Cluniac Order by Walter Fitzalan and is known as the cradle of the Royal House of Stewart. Various styles of architecture from the twelfth to fifteenth centuries are featured in the nave, while the stone-vaulted ceiling of the Choir, with its sculpted bosses, is a fine example of twentieth-century restoration. There is a long tradition of music in the Abbey, and it is a venue for concerts and other special events including its own choir. Worship has been central to the life of the Abbey for over 800 years.

C3 In the centre of Paisley.

ᵂᶜ ♿ ⬤ ⬛ E FREE

🕐 Mon–Sat, 10am–3.30pm;
Sun open for services only.

Tel 0141 889 7654   www.paisleyabbey.org.uk

48 Paisley Museum and Art Galleries

Housed in a neo-classical building, the museum contains displays of important ceramics and nineteenth-century Scottish art. Visitors can learn about old weaving techniques and see the internationally important collection of Paisley shawls and pattern books. The Art Gallery has amongst its collection a large number of paintings by Scottish artists, from Raeburn and Ramsay to the Glasgow Boys, and more recent works.

C3 High Street, centre of Paisley.

ᵂᶜ ♿ ⬛ E FREE

🕐 Tue–Sat, 10am–5pm; Sun 2–5pm;
public holidays, 10am–5pm.

Tel 0141 889 3151   www.renfrewshire.gov.uk

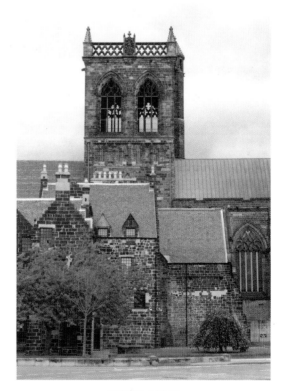

Paisley Abbey

NEW LANARK

The fascinating community of New Lanark nestles by the Falls of Clyde 25 miles southeast of Glasgow and is one of Scotland's most important historic sites, marking where the country first properly embraced the Industrial Revolution. David Dale was a Glasgow merchant banker who founded the complex as a cotton mill in 1785 with the celebrated English cotton engineer Richard Arkwright. But it took Dale's son-in-law Robert Owen, who took over in 1798, to turn New Lanark into a pioneering and highly influential social experiment. Owen, a Welshman, can be said to have created the most enlightened working conditions for Scottish men and women in the early nineteenth century. He pioneered a more human form of capitalism and genuinely believed in the welfare of his workers. As a result he built them a 'planned village' with houses, a school and church to ensure their general comfort and well-being. There was also a co-operative store, a community centre, a day nursery – the world's first – and the slightly sinister-sounding 'Institute for the Formation of Character'. Owen's benign practices as a factory-owner were copied the world over. At its height, New Lanark employed over 2000 men and women in the cotton-spinning process. Robert Owen did not allow children under the age of ten to work in the mill so that they could attend school – he was passionately interested in education being linked to industrial practice. He retired from the business in the 1820s and spread his ideas to the United States, Ireland and to Devon in England. In many ways Owen can be regarded as the founder of trades unionism or the labour movement in politics today. In recent years the buildings in New Lanark have been extensively restored and it is both a living community as well as a popular visitor attraction. New Lanark is now classified as a World Heritage Site. Having viewed the visitor centre and the cotton-spinning premises with actual demonstrations of the machinery, and toured the schoolroom with its slate-boards and tiny desks, visitors can enjoy the magnificent walk to the Falls of Clyde.

49 Palacerigg Country Park ♣ ➡

This park of more than 40 hectares was once windswept moorland, but it now provides a sheltered environment for a variety of wildlife. Visitors can explore the 6 miles of nature trails and walks, or visit the Millennium Longhouses where demonstrations of woodland and other crafts are carried out, such as basket making, charcoal burning, weaving and spinning. Palacerigg also has a collection of rare breeds of both native and farm animals including Scottish wildcat, pine marten, owls and deer, along with sheep and Highland cattle. A children's farm area houses a collection that includes goats, wallabies and a variety of pigs. The ranger service organises a programme of annual events and guided walks.

E4 *Forest Road, Cumbernauld, NE of Glasgow city centre. Signposted off the A8011, Cumbernauld Town Centre road.*

P WC ➡ E ⛱ 🚶 FREE

🕐 Park: open all year, daylight hours.
   Visitor centre: Apr–Sep, 10am–6pm.
   Oct–Mar, 10am–4.30pm.

Tel 01 236 720047   www.northlan.gov.uk

50 Quadmania ★ ✈

A quadbiking centre that offers a number of other outdoor pursuits, including clay-pigeon shooting, canoeing, kayaking, sailing, archery, climbing and gorge walking.

A5 *Blairmore, on W bank of Loch Long; nine miles N of Dunoon on B 833.*

P WC ➡ ♿ ⛱ 🚶 🚶 ♿ £££

🕐 All year round, daily, 9am–dusk.

Tel 01369 810246
www.quadmaniascotland.co.uk

51 Robertson Museum & Aquarium 🏛 ➡

This small Museum opened in 1897 and was based on the original collections of David Robertson, 'The Cumbrae Naturalist'. Both the museum and aquarium are part of the working University Marine Biological Station. The museum highlights the past and present of marine science. The aquarium is dedicated to specimens of Scottish sea life found in the

Clyde sea area, with sea anemones, conger eels, lobsters, crabs, fish and octopus. Smaller tanks contain sea pens, small crustaceans, sea slugs and rock pool inhabitants.

A3 *Millport, Isle of Cumbrae*

P WC ♿ ♿ £

🕐 All year, Mon–Fri, 9am–12.15pm & 1.45pm–4.15pm.
   Jun–Sep, Sat, 10am–1pm & 2pm–4.45pm.

Tel 01475 530581   www.gla.ac.uk/Acad/Marine

52 Sma' Shot Cottages 🏛

These old workers' cottages were rescued and restored by the Old Paisley Society. One focusses on the history of Paisley's weavers in the eighteenth century. Visitors can see working demonstrations on an original loom which was discovered during restoration work in the 1970s. Another cottage recreates the life of a nineteenth-century artisan's home.

C3 *George Place, Paisley.*

WC ➡ ♿ E FREE

🕐 Apr–Sept, Wed & Sat, 12 noon–4pm.

Tel 0141 889 1708   www.smashot.com

53 Strathclyde Country Park ♣ ✈

Strathclyde Country Park is a centre for outdoor recreation. A range of activities are available including watersports, horseriding, fishing, football and orienteering. Mountain bikes are also available for hire. The park's visitor centre and ranger service have information and displays on the history and wildlife of the area. Footpaths and nature trails cover woodland, wetland and open parkland. The park is also home to 'M&D's, Scotland's Theme Park' with its collection of thrill rides including a roller coaster and other entertainments. (The theme park is not free.)

E3 *Hamilton Road, Motherwell, E of Glasgow city centre.*

P WC ♿ ➡ E ⛱ 🚶 🚶 ♿ FREE (park only)

🕐 Park: all year, daily, dawn to dusk, free admission.
   Activities: check website or call for times and charges as these vary with the seasons.

Tel 01698 266155   M&Ds Tel 01698 333777
www.northlan.gov.uk
www.scotlandsthemepark.com

Strathclyde Country Park

54 Summerlee Heritage Park

This major industrial heritage attraction is located on the site of the nineteenth-century Summerlee Ironworks and its branch of the Monklands Canal. It features an electric tramway with rides on modern and Edwardian open-topped trams, and an exhibition hall with working machinery and period room settings. There is also a recreated mine and miners' cottages.

E4 *W of Coatbridge town centre at Heritage Way, off West Canal Street.*

🅿 🚾 ♿ ☕ 🏛 E ☀ 👫 FREE

🕐 Apr–Oct, daily, 10am–5pm.
Nov–Mar, 10am–4pm.

Tel 01236 431261   www.northlan.gov.uk

55 Vikingar!

The Story of the Vikings in Scotland is brought to life via a series of multi-media exhibits. Experience the sights and sounds of life in a Viking Longhouse in 825, while narrators in full costume recount stories of Viking myths and legends.

A3 *Greenock Road, Largs on the A78.*

🅿 🚾 ♿ ☕ ✕ 🏛 E 📺 ♿ ££

🕐 Daily; Apr–Sep, 10.30am–5pm.
Oct–Mar, 10.30am–3.30pm.
Nov–Feb, Sat & Sun only, 10.30am–3.30pm.

Tel 01475 689777
www.vikingar.co.uk

56 Weaver's Cottage

This typical eighteenth-century handloom weaver's cottage houses the last working example of the 800 looms once active in this village in the 1830s. Visitors can try the old skills of weaving, pirn winding and spinning. Upstairs, locally woven shawls and nineteenth-century items are on display. Plants and herbs used to make natural dyes are a feature of the cottage garden.

B3 *M8 J28A, A737, follow signs for Kilbarchan.*

E ££

🕐 1 Apr–30 Sept; daily, 1.30–5.30pm.
Morning visits available for pre-booked groups.

Tel 01505 705588   www.nts.org.uk

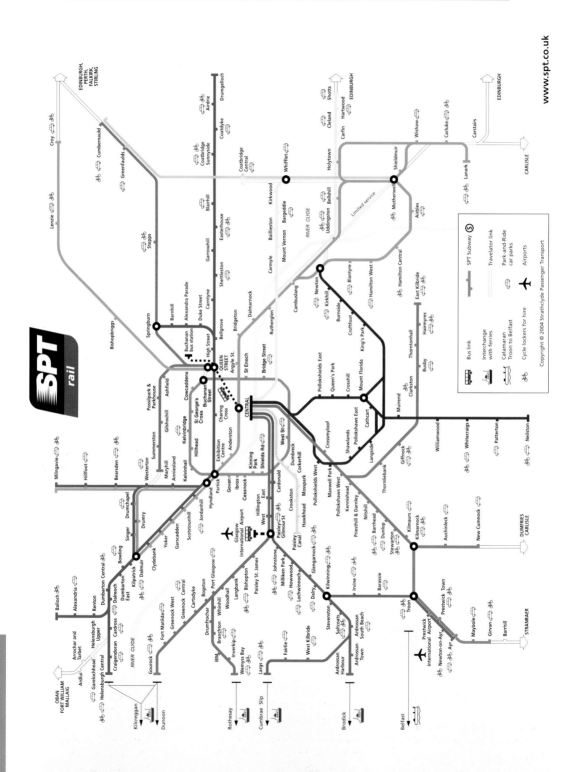

www.spt.co.uk

GENERAL INFORMATION

TRAVEL INFORMATION

Traveline Scotland
Tel: 0870 608 2608   Web: www.travelinescotland.com
Traveline has information for all local public transport
services in Scotland including train, bus, coach and ferry companies.
Traveline also has travel details for people with disabilities.

AIRPORT INFORMATION

Glasgow International Airport is located 8 miles (13 km) from Glasgow city centre with good road access. Regular bus and coach services operate between the airport, the city centre and the national rail network.

Glasgow International
Airport
Arran Court
Paisley PA3 2ST
Tel: 0141 887 1111
Web:
www.baa.com/glasgow

Glasgow Prestwick International Airport is 30 miles (48 km) south-west of Glasgow and can be reached by both road and direct rail link from the city centre.

Glasgow Prestwick
International Airport
Aviation House
Prestwick KA9 2PL
Tel: 01292 511000
Web: www.gpia.co.uk

Glasgow has an excellent network of public transport services throughout the city and surrounding areas with bus and rail services and the advantage of a subway system. The Travel Centre in St Enoch Square and Tourist Information Centres can advise on all aspects on travel in and around Glasgow.

RAIL

National Rail Enquiries
including Scotrail
Tel: 08457 484950
Web:
www.nationalrail.co.uk
www.firstscotrail.co.uk

First ScotRail
Caledonian Chambers
87 Union Street
Glasgow G1 3TA
Tel: Fares & train times
08457 484950
Telesales 08457 550033
Customer Relations
Tel: 0845 601 5929
Web:
www.firstscotrail.co.uk
Email: scotrail.enquiries
@firstgroup.com

Routes: operates within Scotland and also Caledonian Sleepers, which link Aberdeen, Edinburgh, Fort William, Glasgow and Inverness with London

Great North Eastern
Railway Ltd (GNER)
Station Road
York
YO7 6HT
Tel: General sales and enquiries 08457 225 225
Customer Assistance 08457 225 444 (including disabled traveller arrangements)
Customer Relations 08457 225 333
Web: www.gner.co.uk
Email: customercare
@gner.co.uk
Route: operates along Britain's East Coast mainline linking England and Scotland

Virgin Trains
Suite 3/1
Queens House
19 St Vincent Place
Glasgow G1 2DT
Tel: 08457 222 333
Web:
www.virgintrains.co.uk
Route: operates two rail franchises: West Coast Trains and Cross Country Trains. West Coast Trains route include: London Euston-Scotland. Cross Country Trains routes include: Glasgow-Bournemouth, Aberdeen/Dundee-Penzance

Glasgow has two mainline stations within the city connecting with both the national rail network and local areas:

Central Station
Gordon Street
Glasgow
G1 3SL
(for services to the south and west) .

Queen Street Station
Dundas Street
Glasgow
G1 2AF
(for services to the north and east)

SUBWAY
The subway is operated by Strathclyde Passenger Transport (SPT) and is a fast and reliable way of getting around Glasgow's city centre with trains operating every four minutes during peak times. Tickets are available from station ticket offices and ticket machines. Further information on special travel passes can be obtained from any Tourist Information Centre. See map on page 82.

Strathclyde Passenger
Transport (SPT)
Consort House
12 West George Street
Glasgow
G2 1HN
Tel: 0141 332 6811
Web: www.spt.co.uk

BUS & COACH
Buchanan Bus Station is situated north of George Square in the city centre and is Glasgow's main terminal. Local bus services run by First and national coach services by National Express and Scottish Citylink operate from the station. An express service operates to and from Glasgow International Airport on a regular basis.

LOCAL BUSES
First
197 Victoria Road
Glasgow G42 7AD
Tel: 0141 423 6600 for general enquiries and information on tickets and fares:
Web: www.firstgroup.com
Routes: operates an extensive bus network throughout Glasgow with special offers on day and weekly tickets.

COACH
National Express
Tel: 08705 808080
Web:
www.nationalexpress.com

Scottish Citylink Coaches
Buchanan Bus Station
Killermont Street
Glasgow
G2 3NP
Tel: 08705 505050
Web: www.citylink.co.uk
Email: info@citylink.co.uk

*Routes: Glasgow-Aberdeen
Glasgow-Campbeltown
Glasgow-Dumfries
Glasgow-Dundee
Glasgow-Edinburgh
Glasgow-Glasgow Airport
Glasgow-Gourock
Glasgow-Inverness
Glasgow-Isle of Skye
Glasgow-Oban*

TAXIS
Taxis in the city are usually plentiful and the majority will take wheelchairs. They can be hailed in the street, picked up at various ranks or contacted by telephone. Listed below are the telephone numbers of some of the most widely used companies:

Airport Taxi Services
Tel: 0141 848 4900

City Private Hire
Glasgow
Tel: 0141 222 2220

Glasgow Taxis Ltd
Tel: 0141 429 7070

Online Radio Cars
Tel: 0141 550 4040

CAR HIRE
AMK Self Drive
Glasgow
Tel: 0141 950 4200

Arnold Clark
Glasgow
Tel: 0141 334 9501

Avis Rent-A-Car
Glasgow
Tel: 0870 606 0100

Clarkson of Glasgow
Tel: 0141 771 3990

Enterprise Rent-A-Car
Glasgow
Tel: 0141 248 4981

Hertz Rent-A-Car
Glasgow
Tel: 0141 248 7736

Thrifty Car Rental
Tel: 0141 848 5002

PARKING
Glasgow City Council provides over 6000 parking spaces in the city centre, with a further 6000 provided by private companies. Limited off-street parking is also available throughout the city.

WALKWAYS & CYCLE PATHS
Glasgow has some designated cycle lanes but there is a good network of Cycle Routes and Paths within the city and surrounding areas including Glasgow to Loch Lomond Cycleway, Forth & Clyde Canal (Millennium Link), Glasgow to Edinburgh Cycle Route and Clyde Coast Cycle Routes. For more information on cycle routes contact:

Sustrans (Scotland)
162 Fountainbridge
Edinburgh
EH3 9RX
Tel: 0131 624 7660
Email: scotland
@sustrans.org.uk
www.sustrans.org.uk

For further suggestions on cycle routes in the area check the following website:
www.cyclingscotland.com

A local pressure group, Go Bike! have produced a map of cycle routes within the city, they can be contacted on: www.gobike.org

Glasgow has a varied selection of walking routes from guided tours to long distance walkways from the Merchant City Trail to the Clyde Walkway. Footpaths and trails can also be found in many of the country parks around Glasgow. Further information on walking in the area can be found at the Tourist Information Centre.

PLEASE NOTE:
when telephoning from Glasgow, omit 0141 from all numbers. Addresses are all Glasgow unless stated otherwise.

POLICE
Police Stations are located throughout the city.
In an Emergency dial - 999

Strathclyde Police HQ
173 Pitt Street
Glasgow
Tel: 0141 532 200
Web:
www.strathclyde.police.uk

British Transport Police
Tel: 0141 332 3649

LOST PROPERTY
Enquire at the nearest police station or contact the following:

Glasgow Central Station
Tel: 0141 221 8597

First ScotRail
Tel: 0141 335 3276

POST OFFICES
Post Offices are generally open Monday-Friday 9am-5.30pm, Saturday 9am-12 noon and closed Sunday. Some smaller Post Offices maybe closed between 1 and 2pm for lunch and one afternoon mid-week.

Post Office Services
Customer Helpline
Tel: 0845 7223344
Web: www.postoffice.co.uk

City centre branches can be found at the following locations:
St Vincent Street
Merchant City
Bothwell Street
Hope Street
High Street
Charing Cross

MEDICAL INFORMATION

For emergencies: dial 999 - for fire, police or ambulance. Calls are free from any telephone.

For an ordinary illness or a minor accident, your hotel or place of residence can usually put you in touch with a local doctor or dentist.

Glasgow Dental Hospital
Sauchiehall Street
Tel: 0141 211 9600

Glasgow Royal Infirmary
Castle Street
Tel: 0141 211 4000

Southern General Hospital
Govan Road
Tel: 0141 201 1100

Victoria Infirmary
Langside Road
Tel: 0141 201 6000

Western Infirmary
Dumbarton Road
Tel: 0141 211 2000

CATERING FOR DISABILITY IN SCOTLAND

Scotland welcomes visitors with disabilities. There are a number of organisations designed to aid visitors who need advice and information on visiting Scotland.

Capability Scotland is Scotland's primary disability organisation and can offer help and advice for visitors to Scotland. For further information contact:

Advice Service Capability Scotland
11 Ellersly Road
Edinburgh
EH12 6HY
Tel: 0131 313 5510
Web: www.capability-scotland.org.uk
Email: ascs@capability-scotland.org.uk

Glasgow Access Panel has an excellent website which gives information on accessible venues in Glasgow City Centre including accommodation, places of interest and leisure, places of worship, eating out, entertainment, shopping and transport.

Glasgow Access Panel
c/o GCVS
11 Queens Crescent
Glasgow
G4 9AS
Tel: 0141 332 2444
Web: www.glasgowaccesspanel.org.uk
Email: information@gcvs.org.uk

Holiday Care is a national charity and the UK's principal provider of travel advice and information for disabled people and their carers. For further information contact:

Holiday Care
7th Floor
Sunley House
4 Bedford Park
Croydon
CR0 2AP
Tel: 0845 1249971
Web: www.holidaycare.org.uk
Email: info@holidaycare.org

Tripscope also provides information on any aspect of local or national transport for people with disabilities. For further information contact:
Tripscope
The Vassell Centre
Gill Avenue
Bristol
BS16 2QQ
Tel: 0845 758 5641
Web: www.tripscope.org.uk
Email: enquiries@tripscope.org.uk

USEFUL ADDRESSES

VisitScotland
23 Ravelstone Terrace
Edinburgh
EH4 3EU
Tel: 0845 22 55 121
Web: www.visitscotland.com
Email: info@visitscotland.com

CRM Society
The Mackintosh Church at Queen's Cross
870 Garscube Road
Glasgow
G20 7EL
Tel: 0141 946 6600
Web: www.crmsociety.com

Historic Scotland
Longmore House
Salisbury Place
Edinburgh
EH9 1SH
Tel: 0131 668 8800
Web: www.historic-scotland.gov.uk
Email: hsexplorer@scotland.gov.uk

The National Trust for Scotland
Wemyss House
28 Charlotte Square
Edinburgh
EH2 4ET
Tel: 0131 243 9300
Web: www.nts.org.uk
Email: information
@nts.org.uk

RSPB
Scotland Headquarters
Dunedin House
25 Ravelstone Terrace
Edinburgh
EH4 3TP
Tel: 0131 311 6500
Web: www.rspb.org.uk
Email: rspb.scotland
@rspb.org.uk

Scottish Natural Heritage
12 Hope Terrace
Edinburgh
EH9 2AS
Tel: 0131 447 4784
web: www.snh.org.uk
Email: equiries@snh.gov.uk

Scottish Wildlife Trust
Cramond House
Cramond Glebe Road
Edinburgh
EH4 6NS
Tel: 0131 312 7765
Web: www.swt.org.uk
Email: enquiries
@swt.org.uk

Scottish Youth Hostel
Association
7 Glebe Crescent
Stirling
FK8 2JA
Tel: 01786 891400
Web: www.syha.org.uk
Email: info@syha.org.uk

CARAVAN & CAMPING SITES
Craigendmuir Park
Stepps
G33 6AF
Tel: 0141 779 4159
Email: info
@craigendmuir.co.uk
Web:
www.craigendmuir.co.uk

Clyde Muirshiel
Regional Park
Barnbrock Camp Site
Nr Kilbarchan
PA10 2PZ
Tel: 01505 614791
Email: info
@clydemuirshiel.co.uk
Website:
www.clydemuirshiel.co.uk

Lomond Woods
Holiday Park
Tullichewan,
Balloch
Dunbartonshire
G83 8QP
Tel: 01389 755000
Email: lomondwoods
@holiday-parks.co.uk
Web: www.holiday-parks.co.uk

Strathclyde Park Caravan &
Camping Site
366 Hamilton Road
Motherwell
ML1 3ED
Tel: 01698 402 060
Email: strathclydepark
@northlan.gov.uk
Web: www.northlan.gov.uk

ACCOMMODATION
Information and
reservations for Hotels,
Guest Houses and B & Bs
can be obtained from
the Tourist Information
Centres on page 5

BANKS AND BUREAUX DE CHANGE
Most of the banks in the
city will exchange foreign
currency and ATMs
(Automatic Teller Machines)
are widely available.
Normal banking hours
are Monday to Friday
9.30am-4.30pm.

FEXCO
Tourist Information Centre
11 George Square
Tel: 0141 204 4400

American Express Bureaux
de Change
115 Hope Street
Tel: 0141 222 1401

Lunn Poly Bureaux
de Change
Unit 16
Buchanan Galleries
Tel: 0141 331 2482

Thomas Cook Foreign
Exchange
Central Station
Tel: 0141 207 3400

BANKS

Abbey
84 Argyle Street
Tel: 0845 7654321

147-149 Sauchiehall Street
Tel: 0845 7654321

301 St Vincent Street
Tel: 0845 7654321

Alliance & Leicester
1-3 Vincent Place
Tel: 0141 2218707

Bank of Scotland
Central Station
Gordon Street
Tel: 0141 207 9908

Unit 41
St Enoch Centre
Tel: 0141 249 9808

235 Sauchiehall Street
Tel: 0141 531 0500

110 Queen Street
Tel: 0141 207 7400

Clydesdale Bank
7 St Enoch Square
Tel: 0141 221 0951

349 Sauchiehall Street
Tel: 0141 951 7003

Royal Bank of Scotland
22 St Enoch Square
Tel: 0141 248 5726

23 Sauchiehall Street
Tel: 0141 331 2131

10 Gordon Street
Tel: 0141 567 0065

Woolwich
18 Gordon Street
Tel: 0845 071 8192

Allied Irish Bank
227 West George Street
Tel: 0141 226 4421

Bank of Ireland
65 St Vincent Street
Tel: 0141 221 9353

HSBC Bank
120 West Regent Street
Tel: 0845 7404404

BUILDING SOCIETIES

Bradford & Bingley
268 Byres Road
Tel: 0141 334 8149

Britannia Building Society
84 Renfield Road
Tel: 0141 331 2451

Dunfermline Building Society
196 Hope Street
Tel: 0141 332 0845

Nationwide Building Society
19-29 St Vincent Street
Tel: 0141 201 8450

Skipton Building Society
50 Vincent Street
Tel: 0141 226 4112

Yorkshire Building Society
54-58 Gordon Street
Tel: 0845 1200100

PLACES OF WORSHIP

The Glasgow Churches Together website, www.glasgowchurches.org.uk has further information including times of services.

Church of Scotland
Glasgow Cathedral
Castle Street
Tel: 0141 552 6891

Wellington Church
University Avenue
Tel: 0141 339 0454

Baptist
Adelaide Place Baptist Church
209 Bath Street
Tel: 0141 248 4970

Buddhist
Glasgow Buddhist Centre
329 Sauchiehall Street
Tel: 0141 333 0524

Hindu
The Hindu Mandir
1 La Belle Place
Tel: 0141 332 0482

Islamic
Central Mosque
1 Mosque Avenue
Tel: 0141 429 3132

Jewish
Garnethill Synagogue
129 Hill Street
Tel: 0141 332 4151

Methodist
Woodlands Methodist Church
229 Woodlands Road
Tel: 0141 332 7779

Roman Catholic
St Aloysius Church
Garnethill
Rose Street
Tel: 0141 332 3039

St Andrew's Cathedral
90 Dunlop Street
Tel: 0141 221 3096

Scottish Episcopal
St Mary's Cathedral
300 Great Western Road
Tel: 0141 339 6691

ENTERTAINMENT

THEATRES & CONCERT HALLS

The Arches
253 Argyle Street
Box Office: 0870 240 7528
Web: www.thearches.co.uk

CCA
350 Sauchiehall Street
Box Office: 0141 332 7521
Web: www.cca-glasgow.com

Citizens Theatre
119 Gorbals Street
Box Office: 0141 429 0022
Web: www.citz.co.uk

Glasgow Film Theatre
12 Rose Street
Box Office: 0141 332 8128
Web: www.gft.org.uk

Glasgow Royal Concert Hall
2 Sauchiehall Street
Box Office: 0141 353 8000
Web: www.grch.com

Grand Ole Opry
(Glasgow) Ltd
2/4 Govan Road
Box Office: 0141 429 5396

GSC Imax Theatre
Glasgow Science Centre
Pacific Quay
Tel: 0141 420 5000
Web: www.gsc.org.uk

Henry Wood Hall
73 Claremont Street
Tel: 0141 225 3555
Web: www.rsno.org.uk

King's Theatre
297 Bath Street
Tel: 0141 240 1300
Web: www.kings-glasgow.co.uk

Moir Hall & Mitchell
Theatre
6 Granville Street
Charing Cross
Tel: 0141 287 4855

Pavilion Theatre
121 Renfield Street
Tel: 0141 332 1846
Web: www.pavilion
theatre.co.uk

Ramshorn Theatre
University of Strathclyde
98 Ingram Street
Tel: 0141 552 3489

SECC
Glasgow
Tel: 0141 248 3000
Web: www.secc.co.uk

Stand Comedy Club
333 Woodlands Road
Tel: 0870 600 6055
Web: www.thestand.co.uk

Theatre Royal
282 Hope Street
Box Office: 0141 332 9000
Web: www.theatreroyal
glasgow.com

Tramway
25 Albert Drive
Tel: 0141 423 2023
Web: www.tramway.org

Tron Theatre
63 Trongate
Tel: 0141 552 4267
Web: www.tron.co.uk

CINEMAS

GilmorehillG12
9 University Avenue
Tel: 0141 330 5522
Web: www.gilmorehill
g12.co.uk

Grosvenor Cinema
Ashton Lane, Hillhead
Tel: 0141 339 8444
Web: www.grosvenor
cinema.co.uk

Odeon Cinemas
56 Renfield Street
&
Springfield Quay
Paisley Road
Tel: 0870 505 0007
Web: www.odeon.co.uk

Showcase Cinema
Showcase Leisure Park
Coatbridge
Tel: 01236 438000
&
Paisley Business Park
Tel: 0141 887 0011
Web: www.showcase
cinemas.co.uk

UCI (UK) Ltd
Olympia Shopping Centre
East Kilbride
Tel: 01 355 249622
&
Britannia Way
Clydebank
Tel: 0141 951 1949
Web: www.uci-cinemas.co.uk

UGC
The Forge Shopping Centre
Parkhead
Tel: 0871 200 2000
&
Renfrew Street
Tel: 0871 200 2000
Web: www.ugccinemas.co.uk

VUE
Palace Towers
Hamilton
Tel: 08712 240 240
Web: www.myvue.com

ANNUAL EVENTS & FESTIVALS

JANUARY
CELTIC CONNECTIONS – *traditional and celtic music festival*,
Glasgow Royal Concert Hall and other venues

FEBRUARY
NEW TERRITORIES – *contemporary dance, national and international*, Tramway and other venues

MARCH
GLASGOW INTERNATIONAL COMEDY FESTIVAL – various venues

APRIL
GLASGOW ART FAIR + RAW (REAL ART WEEK) – *visual arts*,
George Square, tramway and various venues

MAY
MAYDAZE – *parade, music, dance and entertainment*, Glasgow Green
BIG BIG COUNTRY – *Americana festival*, various venues

JUNE
WEST END FESTIVAL – *festival of music, theatre, exhibitions and carnival*, various venues
LORD PROVOST'S PROCESSION – *parade and visual arts*, George Square

JULY
GLASGOW INTERNATIONAL JAZZ FESTIVAL – George Square and other various venues
GLASGOW MELA – *Asian Arts Festival*, Kelvingrove Park
GLASGOW RIVER FESTIVAL – various venues along the Clyde

AUGUST
GLASGOW INTERNATIONAL PIPING FESTIVAL – *pipe band championships and other events*,
various venues
STRATHAVEN BALLOON FESTIVAL – *hot air balloons and various events*, Strathaven
GREAT SCOTTISH RUN – *half marathon and 10K road races*, Glasgow Green

SEPTEMBER
MERCHANT CITY FESTIVAL – *arts festival*, various venues, Merchant City

NOVEMBER
GLASGAY! – *gay and lesbian arts festival*, various venues
CHRISTMAS LIGHTS – George Square

DECEMBER
WINTER FESTIVAL – various events
HOGMANAY – various outdoor venues

SHOPPING IN GLASGOW

Glasgow is the second-largest retail centre in the UK offering a diverse range of shops and outlets from mainstream high street stores to chic designer boutiques. There is a bustling mixture of traditional shops, modern shopping malls and arcades with bars, cafés and restaurants. The main shopping areas are on Argyle Street, Buchanan Street and Sauchiehall Street, which are right in the city centre. A range of shopping malls including the St Enoch Centre, which is Europe's largest glass structure, and the new Buchanan Galleries, are close to rail, bus and subway services. The Argyle Arcade, built in 1827, contains over 30 jewellers' shops selling both modern and antique jewellery. Princes Square has a number of high-quality shops and a food court and is located just off Buchanan Street. The Italian Centre and Merchant Square are home to famous designer names and stylish cafés and bars.

The West End of Glasgow is home to an array of antique and second-hand shops, selling clothes, books and memorabilia. In the East End is the famous Barras open air market, which is only open on Saturday and Sunday – a must for any bargain hunter and a unique experience.

SHOPPING CENTRES

BUCHANAN GALLERIES SHOPPING CENTRE
Buchanan Street
Tel: 0141 333 9898
www.buchanangalleries.co.uk
Open: Mon-Wed, Fri & Sat, 9am-6pm.
Thur, 9am-8pm. Sun,11am-5pm.
Public Holidays, 11am-6pm.

ST ENOCH SHOPPING CENTRE
55 St Enoch Square
Tel: 0141 204 3900
www.stenoch.com
Open: Mon-Wed & Fri-Sat, 9am-6pm.
Thur, 9am-8pm. Sun,11am-5.30pm.
Public Holidays, 11am-5pm.

ARGYLE ARCADE SHOPPING MALL
30 Buchanan Street
Tel: 0141 221 6680

PRINCES SQUARE SPECIALITY SHOPPING CENTRE
48 Buchanan Street
Tel: 0141 221 0324
www.princessquare.co.uk
Open: Mon-Wed & Fri-Sat, 9.30am-6pm.
Thur, 9.30am-8pm.
Sun,12noon-5pm.

THE BARRAS MARKET
Gallowgate
Tel: 0141 552 4601
Open: Sat & Sun, 10am-5pm

THE ITALIAN CENTRE
John Street/Ingram Street
Tel: 0141 552 6099

MERCHANT SQUARE
71-73 Albion Street
Tel: 0141 552 5908

SPORTING AND LEISURE VENUES

ACTIVITIES
Braehead Skating & Curling Rink
Tel: 0141 885 4611
Web: www.braehead.co.uk

Bedlam Paintball
Tel: 07000 233526
Web: www.bedlam.co.uk

Central Scotland Shooting School
Cumbernauld
Tel: 01324 851672

Glasgow Climbing Centre
Glasgow
Tel: 0141 427 9550
Web: www.glasgowclimbing
centre.co.uk

Scotkart Indoor Karting
Cambuslang
Tel: 0141 641 0222

Scotkart Indoor Karting
Clydebank
Tel: 0141 951 8900
Web: www.scotkart.co.uk

Shandon Country Pursuits
Shandon
Tel: 01436 820838
Web: www.shandoncountry
pursuitsltd.co.uk

ANGLING
Ardgowan Trout Fishery
Greenock
Tel: 01475 522492
Web: www.trout-fishery.co.uk

Carbeth Fishery
Blanefield
Tel: 01360 771006

Dunoon & District Angling Club
Tel: 01369 830350
Web: www.ddac.org.uk

Loch Lomond Angling
Balmaha
Tel: 0141 781 1545
Web: www.lochlomond
angling.com

Lochmill Fishery
Milton of Campsie
Tel: 0141 776 1903

ARCHERY
Shandon Country Pursuits
Shandon
Tel: 01436 820838
Web: www.shandoncountry
pursuitsltd.co.uk

CYCLE HIRE
Alpine Bikes
Glasgow
Tel: 0141 353 2226
Web: www.alpinebikes.co.uk

Dales Cycles
Dobbies Loan
Tel: 0141 332 2705
Web: www.dalescycles.com

Gear Bikes
Hillhead
Tel: 0141 339 1179
Web: www.gearbikess.com

Kinetics
Bearsden
Tel: 0141 942 2552
Web: www.kinetics.org.uk

West End Cycles
16-18 Chancellor Street
Partick
Tel: 0141 357 1344

GOLF
Alexandra Golf Course
Sannox Gardens
Tel: 0141 556 1294

Balmore Golf Club
Torrance
Tel: 01360 620240

Barshaw Golf Club
Paisley
Tel: 0141 889 2908

Bearsden Golf Club
Tel: 0141 586 5300

Bishopbriggs Golf Range
Tel: 0141 762 4883

Blairbeth Golf Club
Rutherglen
Tel: 0141 634 3355

Bonnyton Golf Club
Eaglesham
Tel: 01355 302781

Calderbraes Golf Club
Uddingston
Tel: 01698 813425

Cambuslang Golf Club
Tel: 0141 641 3130

Campsie Golf Club
Lennoxtown
Tel: 01360 310244

Cathcart Castle Golf Club
Clarkston
Tel: 0141 638 0082

Cathkin Braes Golf Club
Rutherglen
Tel: 0141 634 6605

Clober Golf Club
Milngavie
Tel: 0141 956 6963

Clydebank & District Golf Club
Tel: 01389 383831

Coatbridge Golf Course
& Driving Range
Drumpellier Country Park
Tel: 01236 421492

Cowglen Golf Club
Glasgow
Tel: 0141 632 0556

Crow Wood Golf Club
Muirhead
Tel: 0141 779 4954

Douglas Park Golf Club
Bearsden
Tel: 0141 942 2220

Eastwood Golf Club
Newton Mearns
Tel: 01355 500280

Glasgow Golf Club
Bearsden
Tel: 0141 942 2011

Haggs Castle Golf Club
Glasgow
Tel: 0141 427 1157

Hayston Golf Club
Kirtintilloch
Tel: 0141 776 1244

Hilton Park Golf Club
Milngavie
Tel: 0141 956 4657

Kames Golf Club
Cleghorn
Tel: 01555 870015

Kirkhill Golf Club
Cambuslang
Tel: 0141 641 3083

Kirkintilloch Golf Club
Tel: 0141 776 1256

Knightswood Golf Course
Glasgow
Tel: 0141 959 6358

Linn Park Golf Club
Glasgow
Tel: 0141 633 0377

Littlehill Golf Course
Bishopbriggs
Tel: 0141 772 1916

Milngavie Golf Club
Tel: 0141 956 1619

Paisley Golf Club
Tel: 0141 884 3903

Pollok Golf Club
Glasgow
Tel: 0141 632 1080

Ralston Golf Club
Paisley
Tel: 0141 882 1349

Rouken Glen Golf Centre
Glasgow
Tel: 0141 638 7044

Whitecraigs Golf Club
Giffnock
Tel: 0141 639 4530

Windyhill Golf Club
Bearsden
Tel: 0141 942 2349

World of Golf
Clydebank
Tel: 0141 944 4141
Web: www.worldofgolf-uk.co.uk

HORSE RACING
Hamilton Park Racecourse
Bothwell Road, Hamilton
Tel: 01698 283806

HORSE RIDING
Ardgowan Riding Centre
Greenock
Tel: 01475 521390
Web: www.ardgowan-riding.co.uk

Bankhead House Stables
Milngavie
Tel: 0141 956 3798

Easterton Riding School
Mugdock
Tel: 0141 956 1518

Kenmure Riding School
Bishopbriggs
Tel: 0141 772 3041

SPORTS CENTRES
& SWIMMING POOLS
Allander Sports Complex
Bearsden
Tel: 0141 942 2233
Web: www.eastdunbarton. gov.uk

Aquatec
Motherwell
Tel: 01698 332828
Web: www.northlan.gov.uk

Bellahouston Leisure Centre
Glasgow
Tel: 0141 427 9090
Web: www.glasgow.gov.uk

Blantyre Sports Centre
Tel: 01698 821767

Dollan Aqua Centre
East Kilbride
Tel: 01355 260000

Gorbals Leisure Centre
Glasgow
Tel: 0141 429 5556
Web: www.glasgow.gov.uk

Hamilton Water Palace
Tel: 01698 459950

Kelvin Hall International
Sports Arena
Glasgow
Tel: 0141 357 2525
Web:www.glasgow.gov.uk

Lagoon Leisure Centre
Paisley
Tel: 0141 889 4000
Web: www.renfrewshire.gov.uk

Leisuredome
Bishopbriggs
Tel: 0141 772 6391
Web: www.eastdunbarton.goc.uk

North Woodside Leisure Centre
Glasgow
Tel: 0141 332 8012
Web: www.glasgow.gov.uk

Pollok Leisure Pool
Glasgow
Tel: 0141 881 3313

Scotstoun Leisure Centre
Glasgow
Tel: 0141 959 4000
Web: www.glasgow.gov.uk

Sir Matt Busby Sports Complex
Bellshill
Tel: 01698 747466
Web: www.northlan.gov.uk

Strathaven Leisure Centre
Tel: 01357 522820
Web: www.southlanarksire.gov.uk

Time Capsule
Coatbridge
Tel: 01236 449572
Web: www.timecapsule.co.uk

Tollcross Park Leisure Centre
Tel: 0141 763 2345

STADIUMS
Celtic Park
Parkhead
Tel: 0141 556 2611
Web: www.celticfc.net

Firhill Stadium
Maryhill
Tel: 0141 579 1971
Web: www.ptfc.co.uk

Hampden Park
Mount Florida
Tel: 0141 632 1275
Web: www.queensparkfc.co.uk

Ibrox Stadium
Glasgow
Tel: 0870 600 1972
Web: www.rangers.co.uk

ATTRACTION INDEX

● GLASGOW CITY

ATTRACTION INDEX

● AROUND GLASGOW

ALPHABETICAL INDEX

Entries in **bold** indicate photographs

First published in Great Britain in 2005 by
Colin Baxter Photography Limited,
Grantown–on–Spey, PH26 3NA, Scotland

w w w . c o l i n b a x t e r . c o . u k

Photographs copyright © Colin Baxter 2005. Text copyright © Colin Baxter Photography 2005.
Special text features written by Tom-Bruce Gardyne.
Map on page 64 copyright © 2005 Wendy Price Cartographic Services. Based on mapping
by Hallwag, Kümmerley+Frey AG Switzerland. Map on page 82 © Strathclyde Passenger Transport.
Page 39 © Hunterian Museum & Art Gallery, University of Glasgow. Page 50 © courtesy of the
Museum of Transport. Glasgow city plans copyright © XYZ Digital Map Company 2005.

ISBN 1-84107-269-9
Printed in China.

Front cover photograph: *Kelvingrove Art Gallery & Museum*
Back cover photograph: *Tenements, High Street*